Life Cycles - Relationships

DISCOVER CONFLUENCE
IS YOUR RELATIONSHIP FATED?

Neil Killion

Life Cycles Publications

Life Cycles Publications,
Sydney, Australia.

Contact:- lifecyclespublications@gmail.com

ISBN 978-0-6480927-1-1

To lovers, family. friends and colleagues from all over the world.

TABLE OF CONTENTS

PROLOGUE

I want to do something revolutionary in this book. I want to create a new way to look at relationships. This is a logical extension of my totally original theory of life in twelve-year cycles. It is mathematical in structure and has nothing to do with other systems or theories.

My work is based on in-depth biographical analysis, mostly using people with a public profile, so that the data is easily checkable. It has its own terms, both unique and easy to understand, but you will never have heard of them before unless you've read my first two books. Whilst it is not accurate enough to be called a science like physics, it is scientifically based and in no way merely occult.

I write to entertain and I have such a swag of fascinating stories about famous people from throughout history; I guarantee to keep you turning the pages until the very end. I want to show you a brand new concept called "Confluence" and how you can use it to advantage in your own life. I want to redefine what a "Fated Relationship" is and prove it with some of the most famous couples in world history.

Some of you may be mostly concerned with romantic relationships and just who your ideal partner could be. Naturally, it will be addressed, but I don't merely wish to confine myself to one area. All relationships will be examined - love, marriage, family, friendship, career and even your worst enemies. You'll learn a whole new way to evaluate all the important people in your life.

I want to challenge all you trivia buffs. If you know even a fraction of the in-depth knowledge, about the famous and not-so-famous people I cover, I'll be very impressed. I am going to expand the biographical knowledge of all readers exponentially. In fact towards the end, I am literally going to deluge you with facts, so unnervingly accurate, you will be left in no doubt whatsoever about the authenticity of my evidence.

I am now an established theoretician, in that my hundreds of blog articles, two books and over a decade worth of research, are both well-received critically and catalogued in a range of databases. I openly challenge any sceptics or interested academics to prove my evidence is incorrect, something no-one has yet undertaken.

Yet I am a radically different thinker and not part of mainstream scientific/rational wisdom, which asserts all coincidences are merely statistical anomalies to be falsified with a large enough sample.

I welcome you to the living, breathing world of "Life Cycles Theory"; so new that I often conduct my research on an ad hoc basis as I am writing. I publish to spread the word and to get you excited about looking with fresh eyes at your own life and the lives of others and the many miracles that may be contained therein.

CHAPTER ONE

THE REVOLUTION CONTINUES

Ever since Book Two, *The Life Cycles Revolution* was published right at the end of the 2012 year, I began to see a continued trend in the critical success of what I was doing. A high average in my professional reviews and a couple of finalist awards culminated in receiving the Silver Medal in the Philosophy/Religion section of an international contest. Even more satisfying was the timbre of some sections of the reviews. Comments such as:

- *"This book is extraordinary. Reading it has the power to change someone's life completely."*

- *"A must read for anyone who wants to understand the meaning of life."*

- *"The book puts together enough evidence to make Killion's thesis credible...in a way that will keep readers hooked."*

It indicated to me that my essential message was getting through.

However all this affirmation did not mean I sat back and basked in the moment for long. For me, the pioneer of the youngest theory of life; it simply meant that without any pause, I had to keep pushing forward. So the research and writing of my, by now, numerous blog posts and articles continued on schedule.

You see, to this day, I still feel a little doubtful, that I will be able to drive onwards with good quality biographical case histories. There is a part of me that always needs convincing that I am, indeed, on the right path. It is, by the way, the most single-minded path you could imagine amongst a multitude of new thinking generally and particularly for those who have written about patterns within lives.

Why do I make this claim? It's because I know I travel alone. There is no-one else who looks at life as I do. I've checked and rechecked all available sources and apart from the completely unproven occult systems; there are others such as the psychologists Erik Erikson, Roger Gould and Daniel

Levinson, who have published acknowledged texts about life in stages.

Yet they do not use a true cycle theory, with exact parameters and definitions. Their conclusions are drawn from a linear view of life and they are much more liberal with their time periods. New stages can be ushered in over several years (i.e., before or after their nominal date of commencement); all of which makes exact measurement impossible.

I radically propose a cycle view of life, with parameters so exact, it is sometimes down to the same month/week of events 12 years apart. Much more like a mechanistic model. Most importantly, from my perspective, I have arrived at my current position without any preconceived links. I thus have no known cause for my results. Therefore the maxim that 'correlation does not prove causation' doesn't apply to me.

So, for instance, in the occult world there is this totally unprovable connection between a period of around 12 years (11.8618 years to be exact), that the planet Jupiter takes to orbit the Sun and our behaviour. This supposition is without any scientific foundation. What's worse, it's also without any detailed case history support.

I have written a much longer article on this subject and I only managed to find one hapless astrologer, who gave the lamest, most obviously post hoc examples. For instance, she said that because she got pregnant when she was in (or around I'm not sure) her age 24 year, it had something to do with Jupiter's size (it is the largest planet). She stated because Jupiter was expansive and she suddenly expanded, there was a connection. Really!? I'd hate to see what a sceptic or rationalist would make of this.

The numerological connection of a period of 7 years, representing change and a new direction, is similarly flawed. All I had to do is take one of their supposed important years of change (i.e., the mid-life age of 35) and investigate what a number of their interpretations were.

Let me tell you, without going into a lot of detail, they were all wildly different with almost no common ground. What's worse, we ended up with the same looseness of definition that all others seemed to share. That is, without supplying any case history detail, they said that this new era can come upon us a couple of years prior to or after the median age of 35. It is all totally untestable waffle.

My "Life Cycles Theory" was derived from the pioneering work of the prominent psychologist Daniel Levinson. He wrote the book *The Seasons Of A Man's Life* (1978), which looked at a career development model for adult males. He studied a group of only 12 white-collar male managers/professionals over a 20-year period to come up with his model for career development.

He had very straightforward accompanying terminology, (which included phrases like the 'Mid-Career Identity' also called the 'BOOM-i.e., be one's own man-AGE' and the well-known term 'Mid-Life Crisis'). I used his model in my work as a mid-career counsellor and CEO and founder of my own outplacement company.

When I decided to do an ad hoc research project on the validity of his 'Mid-Career Identity' timescale (which was meant to be ushered in the mid-to-late 30s), I accidentally found a much tighter correlation with just one year (the age of 36), than I ever expected. Not just the ushering in of a new and important stage of one's mid-career, sometime between the ages of 35 to 39, but a strange event I labelled the "Age 36 Phenomenon". Events in this one year often came to dominate a person's whole career and life, in a way which was unmistakable.

Much later I discovered a similar close fit with the age of 24 and the beginning of what Levinson called the 'First Career Identity'. Levinson was perfectly happy to see this stage of life happen on a continuum of a person's young adulthood (between the ages of 25 to 29 give or take). In exactly the same way, I might add, as leading theorist Roger Gould, author of the landmark book *Transformations* (1979), called his first adult developmental stage 'Getting Into The Adult World' (sometime between ages 22 to 28).

Not for me, however, these reasonable and well-argued new developmental stages of a young adult's life. No, what I saw was a radically new view of exact and precise correlations of events twelve years apart. When I wrote *The Life Cycles Revolution* I included a detailed test using the well-known and documented life of Napoleon Bonaparte. If he had a major career breakthrough moment in his age 36 year (which, by his own admission, was the proudest moment of his entire life), did it correlate with any similar type of event/s in his age 24 year? It's an exact and testable hypothesis.

You can read the details in the book if you wish, but I found a similar major career breakthrough moment in young Napoleon's life when he was 24. An event quite startlingly similar in nature to his famous victory at the Battle of Austerlitz, when he was 36. One which got him promoted from an Artillery

Major to Brigadier-General. Not only that, but it happened, within a matter of a week or so, at the same time as Austerlitz did 12 years later. Crazy, isn't it? Welcome to my brave new world!

Then, my next discovery came along, when I started to document many cases of sudden and dramatic change occurring in an age 24 or 36 year. I found a trend of a person's whole life being altered by events happening in just one day. I discovered all sorts of different cases; such as where TV marketing guru Joy Mangano (subject of the film *Joy* starring Jennifer Lawrence) overcame a bad case of stage fright, when the bright TV lights were on her for the first time. It was the pivotal moment of the film and began her true career and it happened when she was in her age 36 year.

Totally different was the case of well-known crime author Patricia Cornwell, who was almost killed in a car accident at 36, but realised that her life was generally out of control and made a life-changing new start.

These and many more like them caused me to start using the phrase the "One Day Phenomenon". As you can see, all my terms are straightforward and logical. I purposely don't use anything that sounds abstruse, nor take an academic approach to my method. There's no smoke and mirrors surrounding "Life Cycles Theory". It's accessible to all and easy to follow.

To further compound my research, I also began to follow the similarity of both the timing and the nature of events, that occurred over all the adult twelve-year interval ages, that I could study in a person's life. In a landmark case, I applied this to the life and career of Barack Obama. I was able to show essentially the same initiatives related to health care issues and legislation, that took place during his age 24, age 36 and finally (with the Affordable Health Care Act) at 48. The only difference was the sphere of influence.

The first instance was to do with the City of Chicago, the second the State Legislature of Illinois and lastly as President. But, of even more significance to me, was the fact that they all took place at a similar time of the year. The best I could ascertain was most probably within the same month. I called this phenomenon the "Alignment Of The Dates".

So can you see for yourselves how far removed I am from all other theorists and definitely from the occult systems? For example, Erik Eriksson, who was the pioneer of an adult psychosocial model of development, took the broadest possible first adult period with the ages of 18 to 40.

He stated that the crisis to be addressed was intimacy versus isolation, with the goal of forming and consolidating an affectionate relationship. This is fine within his context, but very broad-brush in style and so much different to my biographical analysis model.

I am not really happy until I have found the most specific instances of noteworthy and sometimes life-changing events, within a very narrow framework. Also, my research inclines me to conclude, that we are not so much looking at a linear cradle to grave view of life divided into stages; but a symbolic twelve-year cycle, with the same themes getting repeated.

When I wrote *The Life Cycles Revolution*, I touched on the subject of relationships in passing and it occurred to me that since this was always going to be my next book - my next progression with the theory - I should devote a fair bit of time to researching and exploring cases of very well-known couples.

I began by exploring some all-time celebrated love matches, such as Bogie and Bacall, Taylor and Burton, etc. I really wanted to know how they might correlate with my "Life Cycles Theory" and if there was some way of understanding what made the lifelong, grand passion of Bogie and Bacall measurable against the turbulent and ultimately doomed, shorter-term Burton-Taylor match. Interestingly, Liz and Richard are held up in marriage guidance counselling as the model of a 'couldn't live with each other and couldn't live without' couple.

Slowly I began to see a pattern with quite a few cases, which gave me a possible answer to this question. I tested it out with real situations that were playing out in my subject's lives as I wrote about them. No better way to learn than in the ever-constant laboratory of life.

Then, after a time, I realised I had been too narrow in my coverage of the all-encompassing topic of relationships. I turned my attention to significant friendships, where both people had been going through transformative episodes in their lives together.

A good example is the case of well-known actors Leonard Nimoy and William Shatner, who came together with the making of *Star Trek*, but remained the closest of friends until Leonard's recent death. This is such a wonderful story and I'll be covering it in full as we go. Next I discovered, that the friendship component of relationships could be so strong, that it outlasted a marriage or romance between a couple. I'll examine this with several well-known cases.

Also work relationships were studied using "Life Cycles Theory" to see the potential for some people, who share significant experiences together, having the extra bonds of friendship and empathy, that the theory predicts should happen. We'll be visiting a number of cases, but one which you all know well, will be the 1969 moon landing with Armstrong, Aldrin and Collins. I plan, as I always do, to uncover some interesting and lesser-known facts about my subject's lives.

A major focus of my research has also been relationships in families. A good example, which I'll cover, will be the very famous Wright Brothers. This is such an interesting topic area with so many possibilities. My prime focus has been between generations and specifically between fathers and sons.

However, unlike my mentor Levinson, I am equally interested in female case studies and I have consistently included their profiles. In fact, all lives interest me, the only reason I focus on celebrity lives is simply that their details are on the public record, which can be verified by anyone. Also, I find it easier to discuss lives which are broadly known and don't need much introduction.

Oddly enough, my attention was accidentally drawn to the element of fate in relationships, where the other person turns out to be your worst enemy rather than your best friend. Sometimes people encounter this for only a period of their lives, such as an election or a battle, and sometimes it is the result of your lives being tied together over many years. Once again my analysis will uncover some interesting examples.

Speaking of uncovering some otherwise hidden or lesser known facts, I have made some extraordinary discoveries whilst doing my in-depth biographical analyses, the real story behind the glossy summary of a person's highlights. Mind you, I didn't go searching for these stories, but because of the small number of years I study in great detail, I have inadvertently revealed the truth warts and all.

For example, in the case of Mary Queen of Scots, I discovered recent forensic evidence, which makes her infamous age 24 year even blacker. The same result for this year with Charles Dickens, where recently discovered letters highlighted the still unresolved claim, that he drove the eminent illustrator of the *Pickwick Papers*, Robert Seymour, to suicide by hijacking the project.

Or that populist journalist and author, Gail Sheehy, was successfully sued over allegations she plagiarised the then-unpublished work of Roger Gould, to write her best-selling book *Passages*. Or just who wrote the all-time bestse-ller *To Kill A Mockingbird*? This is not my main game, of course, but I come across it nonetheless. It has led me to use a phrase to describe my work as, 'psycho-biography with a twist'.

In fact, I'm going to illustrate this process now and show how "Life Cycles Theory" differs from all others, by briefly illustrating with the life of one of the main protagonists of this chapter; the well-known psychologist, Erik Erikson. Apart from glossy entries in biographic summaries, describing him as being known for his eight stage theory of psychosocial development and for coining the now-common term 'identity crisis', what do we really know about him?

I mean, he served as professor at universities such as Harvard and Yale, was the twelfth most cited psychologist of the twentieth century and studied psychoanalysis under Sigmund and Anna Freud...but did you also know he lacked any university qualification whatsoever! After scraping through high school, he studied at Art College for a short time, before dropping out and literally wandering around areas of Europe as a bohemian and would-be artist for some seven years. There just has to be a story here doesn't there?

My only question is, "does it have any relevance to events that happened to him in his age 24 year, which in his case is June 15, 1926 to June 15, 1927?" Also, could it be traced to one fateful day in this twelve-month period, when something fundamentally changed his life? Not only that but can such an event be linked to other major breakthrough moments, which occurred in his life at subsequent 12-year intervals (i.e., at 36 and 48)?

Finally, is it possible to align the dates of the events occurring during these years, which is quite difficult without very specific information? So I think you'll agree, I'm nothing if not exact and uncompromising and when you think about it, downright preposterous, in my assumption of a silent mechanistic structure underlying life. Particularly if you compared it to the rational and scientific view, of life being a random and unplanned flow of events and dismissing all coincidences as not being significant.

Let's now rejoin Erik on his unplanned journey. This story has a lot to do with just one other person, who was about to connect the young Erik Erikson to a world he didn't know existed. One that would become like a Pandora's Box for him and open up his first adult career identity and fundamentally change his life forever. That person was his only close friend, Peter Blos, whom he had known since school. They bonded because they both had a Gentile father and a Jewish mother; although Erikson never knew his father or what his real surname was. His whole life was to become a quest to resolve his own identity crisis.

In 1926, however, all Erik knew was that he would never become a successful artist and he returned to Vienna to become an art teacher instead. He used to do child portraits to supplement the money his mother would occasionally send to him.

By contrast, Peter's career had taken a much more conventional path. He had just graduated from Heidelberg University as a teacher in 1925 and was introduced to Anna Freud (youngest daughter of Sigmund), by a family friend, Eva Rosenfeld. Anna, in turn, recommended him as a tutor to Bob Burlingham (son of the US-born Dorothy Burlingham, who was in analysis with Anna).

He began this role using Eva's house as a classroom in 1926. OK, let's now join the dots. Peter was due to go on holidays over the summer of 1927, so he decided to recommend his old friend Erik as a replacement and wrote to tell him of this. When would this have been?

It had to be prior to summer and thus still within Erik's age 24 year. There would have been a day (not precisely known) when he read and decided to accept this offer that would ultimately come to change his life forever. At first, he began by just doing sketches of Dorothy's children, but he was soon given the job as their assistant tutor. He then impressed Anna, to the extent that he began to learn psycho-analysis, through being her patient and later meeting with Sigmund in the process.

It really was a case of being in the right place at the right time. This breakthrough moment in an age 24/36 or 48 year is what I look for in every biographical analysis I do. Not within a loosely defined number of years or number of events, but a tightly defined formula, that forms the basis of other hypotheses for my subject's life.

Speaking of this process in Erik's subsequent twelve-year intervals, let's do it now. I have previously written about him in *The Life Cycles Revolution*, so I'll be brief here. When Erik was aged exactly 36, he began a study of children on a Sioux reservation and how they coped with the difficulties of the passage to adulthood in a culture, that was itself under threat.

This began Erikson's theory of an 'identity crisis', for which he is famously known. Again, unfortunately, I can't say exactly when such a breakthrough moment may have occurred and if it was aligned with when he received the letter from Peter Blos twelve years previously, but it did happen precisely on schedule. Then, when he was aged 48, he published his first and most important book *Childhood and Society*, following on with the twelve-year cycle model like clockwork.

Now contrast this with Erikson's own eight stage theory. Apparently later in his career, he sought to dispense with the notion of stipulating a period of years, altogether. Instead, he said the aim of each stage was to experience the highs and lows of the particular spectrum for the stage we are in, and then achieve a positive outcome he called a 'virtue'.

So, for example, in our younger adult years (nominally the ages of 18 to 40), we are meant to experience feelings of isolation and rejection and then find commitment and contentment in a relationship and thus come out the other end with a satisfactory resolution or 'virtue'.

I have no issues with the implied getting of wisdom message, but I beg to differ by pointing out that sweeping generalisations can miss out entirely on the realities of everyday life. This model can't and doesn't fit most lives. We don't suddenly turn around at 40 or any particular age and say to ourselves, "that's it, I've now experienced the highs and lows (in this case of love) and I've worked it out and I'm moving on."

Successful long term relationships still experience highs and lows all the time; relationships can dissolve all the time and people can fall madly in love, without a thought for the consequences, all the time. People within relationships can still feel isolated and rejected and get depressed.

Contrast this with my radical new view of life, which says there is not only some benign type of determinism that operates within our lives, in spite of our acknowledged free will; but it has a most unusual and precise formula based on a twelve-year cycle. It is a testable model and hundreds and hundreds of casework examples have been assembled.

Most importantly it appears to confirm, that what we are doing is repeating a newer version of the theme of all previous twelve-year cycles that we've lived through. So for me, life's a cycle, not a series of stages.

So now you know how different I am from all other theorists. I want to show you how this works when we start to analyse profiles for couples and sometimes even small groups. The time frames get even more compressed and precise, and the conclusions get even more original than the basic theory.

I can guarantee you've never viewed love and friendship and family relations this way before. Once again, you don't have to believe me, all I ask for is an open mind when you begin to explore the many celebrity lives we are going to analyse.

This journey is one you are taking with me now, but it is also one I have been on for over four years since the publication of my last book. I am very pleased to have you join me as we journey together...

CHAPTER TWO

LIFE CYCLES BASIC THEORY

I have to apologise to readers, who may already be somewhat familiar with my key concepts, but I always have to assume that this would be the first time people have heard of the theory, or of me. Because I've introduced the complete theory in *The Life Cycles Revolution*, I'm not going to double up here. I'm simply going to give an outline of all you might need to know, before I get into my subject of "Life Cycles - Relationships" in the next chapter.

These days, people seem to like shortened versions of things in general; short messages, shortened words, 10-second sound bites and the like. In particular, it seems important to be able to encapsulate your main idea in a three-word phrase and I would be able to oblige when asked what exactly "Life Cycles Theory" is all about. The answer is simply, "twelve-year cycles".

I have also been asked to summarise my ideas in one sentence, so the slightly expanded version would be, "a theory of life in twelve-year symbolic cycles, based on detailed biographical evidence and not related to the occult."

Now, of course, there's quite a bit more to it and the full theory contains 44 new terms and icons that cover all areas. This time around I just want to deal with the three main concepts and give first-time readers a chance to get better acquainted. So, in order to get started, I'm going to outline the basis of each of the three.

The first is the name I give to the beginning year in each new twelve-year cycle (the ages of 12, 24, 36, 48, etc.). I use the term the "Year of Revolution", because it seems to me to literally amount to a revolution in your life. It's like a new beginning and it causes upheaval in one form or another; something most of us would prefer not to have. Also, it contains moments where we do not feel fully in control of the outcome.

I was not merely content to search for achievements and new eras either, I began to study just how this process works within the allotted twelve-month period. It was then I uncovered a two stage process for this revolution in our lives. The first was a distinct low point that equated to the symbolic death of the old cycle. In honor of one of my earliest famous people profiles, Napoleon, I gave it the name the "Trafalgar Moment".

This was because during his age 36 "Year of Revolution", he initially suffered his worst-ever naval defeat at the hands of Horatio Nelson. However subsequently, I have used a more generic description, calling it simply the "Moment of Frustration/Setback". My basic point is that things are usually going to get worse before they get better.

The second stage was originally called the "Austerlitz Moment", again in honor of Napoleon's celebrated victory over two other empires in just one day. In the same way, as I have just shown, these days I use the generic phrase the "Moment of Breakthrough/Achievement".

I describe it as accompanied by a heightened state of euphoria, which some individuals have likened to falling in love. The better known the public record case history, the easier it is to show people just what I mean.

Let me illustrate with one of my many current case studies. I often make a habit of analysing celebrity deaths, because I have no control over who is on this list and therefore it forms a 'blind study' of who my subjects are. The recent death of legendary boxer Muhammad Ali led me to study his age 36 "Year of Revolution".

Without any prior detailed knowledge of his boxing career, I discovered his "Moment of Frustration/Setback". It was when he very unexpectedly lost his heavyweight title to newcomer Leon Spinks in a controversial split-decision, only two months past his age 36 birthday. Spinks had only been in seven fights and this was called, "the worst defeat of Ali's career".

Couldn't be any clearer, could it? Ali had fought many close battles in recent times, with the likes of George Foreman and Joe Frazier, only to be beaten by a veritable kid. However, he was described as out of shape before this fight. Then he goes through a process of rigorous training and preparation and around six months later he clearly beats Spinks, to become the first boxer in history to hold the title on three separate occasions.

This is his "Moment of Breakthrough/ Achievement". He declares it will be his last fight and he rightly lays claim to calling himself, "the best of all-time". So how do you think he must have felt that night? Really happy? Euphoric, I'm sure.

His reputation is redeemed and it happened on one single night of his life.

Of course, I do acknowledge that money troubles, some two years down the track, caused him to take an ill-advised fight against Larry Holmes, but in September, 1978, he had it all.

This also shows the principle, that certain key years are like golden opportunities, but with free will operating you can still do anything you like at any time. These years of golden opportunity, however, as you have just seen, will carry a heavier weight of destiny than at other times. At day's end, his ignominious loss isn't particularly remembered. Being the only three-time champion was what really mattered for his legacy.

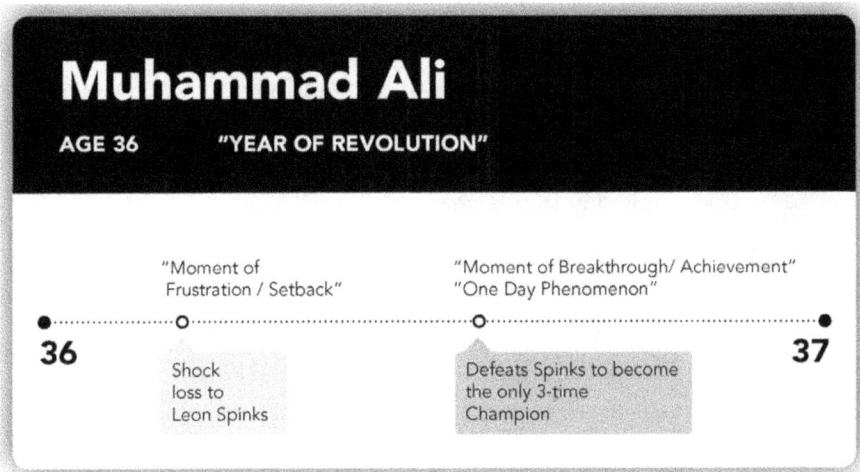

Muhammad Ali

AGE 36   **"YEAR OF REVOLUTION"**

"Moment of Frustration / Setback"	"Moment of Breakthrough/ Achievement" "One Day Phenomenon"
36 ○	○ **37**
Shock loss to Leon Spinks	Defeats Spinks to become the only 3-time Champion

I hope you're getting the picture so far because I'm about to move on to the second concept. During my early research, I noticed that there was one more important year of change in the twelve-year cycle. This occurred seven years after the "Year of Revolution" and it involved both direction change and some form of uphill challenge, to cope with the new circumstances. I gave this the name the "Year of Broken Pathways". As before, the name says it all, because your pathway literally seems to break in some form during this time. This corresponds to the years 7, 19, 31, 43, etc.

Again, this concept is most easily understood with Napoleon's life. If he had his most famous victory at 36, which effectively gave him control of Europe, what highly significant event happened to him seven years later at age 43? If you are scratching your head at this point I'll help out, by saying that the battles of Trafalgar and Austerlitz both happened in the second half of the year 1805. So if you add seven to this what year do you get? Yes, it's 1812, and we all know what happened then, don't we?

This time his path was well and truly broken when he made the ill-fated decision to invade Russia with winter coming on. In spite of a number of victories, he suffered huge losses with around 90% of his army wiped out or deserted. His challenge and uphill struggle was obvious; he had to try and hold onto what remained of his empire in Europe.

Same as we did last time, I'll take a more contemporary example, that again is widely known. This time we'll look at the life of world renowned statesman, Nelson Mandela. When he was 36, he made an early and significant mark in his career, when he was prominent in the adoption of the Freedom Charter at a conference attended by some 3,000 delegates in Kliptown. This called for democracy and human rights and commitment to a non-racial South Africa. It was, as you know, to become his life's work; so once again the central importance of this one year in Mandela's long life is corroborated. It also happened on one single day in this year.

The next question we have to ask is, "what event/s might have taken place some seven years down the track when Nelson was aged 43?" In his age 43 "Year of Broken Pathways", after many years of peaceful resistance had not produced change, he adopted guerrilla tactics of attacking a few government installations; in his role as commander of the military wing of the ANC, known as the Spear of the Nation. It should be noted that these attacks were not designed to endanger any lives and were carried out at night.

When Mandela was underground during this time he wrote the famous words, "the struggle is my life. I will continue fighting for freedom till the end of my days." So this transformation, from peaceful rhetoric to direct action, is how his pathway gets broken and it is obvious he has an uphill challenge on his hands. Not too long after this he gets caught and convicted and receives a sentence of 27 years in prison.

Can you see how very straightforward this conclusion is? Yet these prominent events in the life history of Mandela could have happened at any time, couldn't they? If they were merely aspects of developmental stages, or part of the random flow of life, then they could have happened at any age or say, during a nominal period of five or seven or more years.

But they didn't, did they? These events occurred on time during Mandela's age 36 and age 43 years and at the same time meeting the exact definitions of "Life Cycles Theory". So you have now been introduced to these two important years in the twelve-year cycle. They represent the first and the eighth years and the seven year period between them is known as the period of "Unbroken Forward Momentum". This is because the theme that gets ushered in during a "Year of Revolution" proceeds more or less in a straight line for the next seven years.

So, Napoleon effectively conquers Europe in one day during his age 36 "Year of Revolution" and runs his Empire for some seven years, until things change in a big way during his age 43 "Year of Broken Pathways", with the ill-fated Russian invasion. On the other hand, Nelson Mandela becomes a statesman for getting the ANC to adopt the Freedom Charter in one day in his age 36 "Year of Revolution".

Next, he pursues a path of peaceful resistance for some seven years, until he becomes frustrated with his lack of progress and increasing government-backed violence and then things change in a big way, when he adopts guerrilla tactics by attacking some government buildings during his age 43 "Year of Broken Pathways".

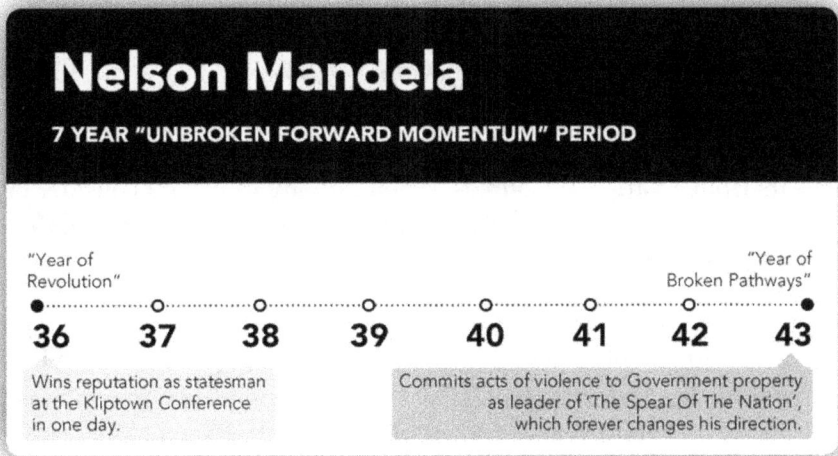

Nelson Mandela

7 YEAR "UNBROKEN FORWARD MOMENTUM" PERIOD

"Year of Revolution"   "Year of Broken Pathways"

36	37	38	39	40	41	42	43

Wins reputation as statesman at the Kliptown Conference in one day.

Commits acts of violence to Government property as leader of 'The Spear Of The Nation', which forever changes his direction.

You will also observe that where I can, I like to get an actual quote from the person themselves, as they talk about the effect some of these events have on them. This is what I refer to as "Subjective Evidence" i.e., from the subject. It reinforces my assertions in a way that is difficult to dispute.

For instance, Napoleon himself said that winning the Battle of Austerlitz was the proudest moment of his career. Muhammad Ali made a similar quote during his age 36 "Year of Revolution" when he announced he would go out on a high by becoming the first (and still only) boxer to hold the heavyweight crown on three separate occasions. It would also avenge his shock loss to Leon Spinks earlier that same year.

The other type of evidence I search for is "Objective Evidence". This consists of reports by commentators, journalists, historians and researchers in general. Wherever there is widespread agreement, by a number of reputable sources, then I know my evidence stands on solid ground. For all my many analyses, I make a point of checking and rechecking my facts. In this regard, I stand in stark contrast to all other theories of life.

Now that I've presented an overview of my only two important years for study in the twelve-year cycle, I would like to introduce my third and last basic concept of "Life Cycles Theory". This is the integration of all my data into one summary chart, known as a "Life Chart". I call the "Years of Revolution" and the "Years of Broken Pathway" in a person's life the "Significant Years". These amount to the ages of 7, 12, 19, 24, 31, 36, 43, 48, 55, 60, etc. It's just arithmetic really, you take each twelfth year (which is a "Year of Revolution") and then add seven to this to get the associated "Year of Broken Pathway".

This may be easily said, but believe me, it takes a lot of work to provide such a comprehensive analysis. You can also see that I must usually work with a famous (or at least very newsworthy) individual to be able to research all these years from a variety of sources. When I do my research I consider myself to be like a latter-day Eliot Ness, fossicking through the files and paperwork to get at the likely truth, rather than the glossy outward presentation.

When I have gathered all my data, I then make a condensed statement for each of the "Significant Years", that is entered into a spreadsheet-style chart. Now comes the hardest part of all. I have to look for similarities in the essential themes for each of the "Years of Revolution" and then separately for each of the "Years of Broken Pathway". This is where the straightforward nature of the theory becomes complex. What I am looking for is verifiable similarities between important events in each separate twelve-year cycle.

So, in Mandela's case, we have him becoming a recognised statesman for the ANC at the well-known Kliptown Conference in his age 36 "Year of Revolution"; so in what way could this be compared to events in his age 24 "Year of Revolution"? Again it's a testable hypothesis. When he was in his age 24 "Year of Revolution", he joined the ANC as an activist. It marked the formal commencement of his political career. This comparison is very easy to discern. It is almost the same type of event, relating to his formal political career.

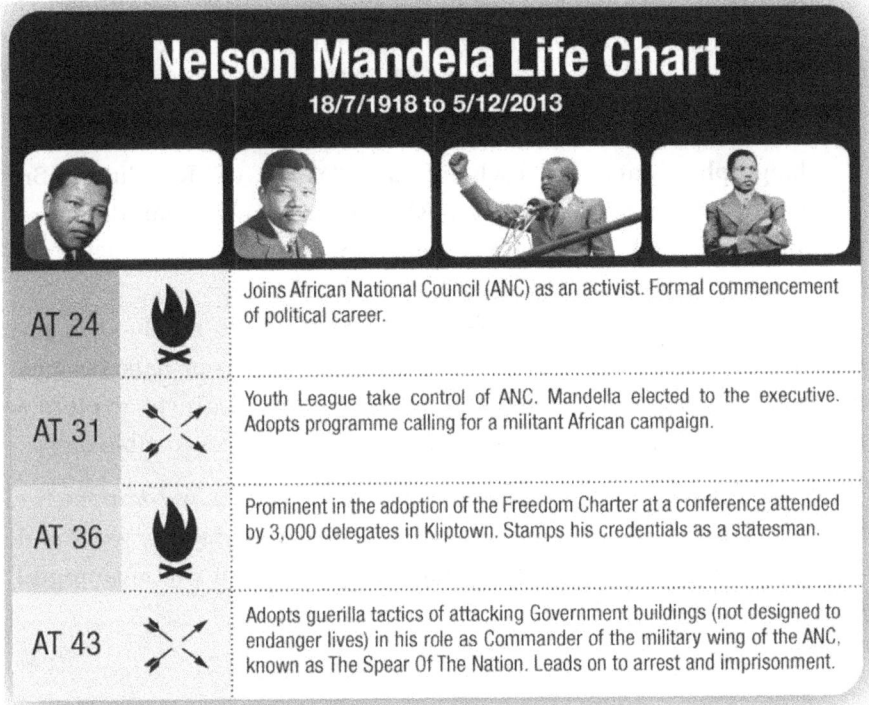

Nelson Mandela Life Chart
18/7/1918 to 5/12/2013

AT 24		Joins African National Council (ANC) as an activist. Formal commencement of political career.
AT 31		Youth League take control of ANC. Mandella elected to the executive. Adopts programme calling for a militant African campaign.
AT 36		Prominent in the adoption of the Freedom Charter at a conference attended by 3,000 delegates in Kliptown. Stamps his credentials as a statesman.
AT 43		Adopts guerilla tactics of attacking Government buildings (not designed to endanger lives) in his role as Commander of the military wing of the ANC, known as The Spear Of The Nation. Leads on to arrest and imprisonment.

This is what I have called "Substantive Similarity", as opposed to other examples, called "Symbolic Similarity", where I have to look at more general underlying themes. As I examine each subsequent "Year of Revolution" or "Year of Broken Pathway" in my subject's life, I have to try to keep coming up with related events, that meet the definition of these years.

Now, you can see for yourselves, that not only are my most basic premises precise and totally different to anything else, but if you add this level of complexity, it is so far beyond the realms of mere chance occurrence, or strange coincidence, as to be a virtual statistical impossibility. That is, of course, if you take a totally rational/scientific view.

Therefore, in summary, the three basic concepts of "Life Cycles Theory" are :

1. The "Year of Revolution"- This is the first year of the twelve-year cycle and equates to the ages of 12, 24, 36, 48, 60, etc. It is marked by important new beginnings and achievements, through a process of

sudden upheaval, rather than a smooth transition.

2. The "Year of Broken Pathway"- This occurs seven years after the "Year of Revolution" and equates to the ages of 7, 19, 31, 43, 55, etc. This is marked by a direction change and uphill challenge. It implies that the path you have been on gets altered and you cannot return to it.

3. The "Life Chart"- This is a spreadsheet-style compilation of all the biographic data for each of the "Years of Revolution/Broken Pathway". It also contains a short-form phrase that describes the similarities of the underlying themes for each.

I hope you can now appreciate all the complexities involved in putting together a full "Life Chart". Well if you can, hold onto your hats, because I'm going to get even more precise and complex, as I begin to explore what happens when we try to overlap two "Life Charts" with compatible dates.

This is the new world of "Confluence" and it defines my approach to all manner of relationships - romance, marriage, friendship, family, work and any others that bring two people, or sometimes more, into a meaningful co-existence.

CHAPTER THREE

INTRODUCING CONFLUENCE

Having properly prepared the groundwork, it is now time to introduce the central thesis of this book. It is the concept called "Confluence". I'm sure you will find it an easy-to-understand term. My definition is an overlap of the "Significant Years" shared by two or more individuals in some form of relationship. Let's explore what this means.

If you take the most straightforward example, let's say that you and your partner were both born in the same calendar year. For instance, you were born in May and he/she was born in September. This would mean that when you were both 12 years old (i.e., the first common "Year of Revolution" after birth) you and he/she would share the period between September of that year and May of the next in common. That is a total of 8 months out of a possible 12. Moreover, this same formula would apply to every single "Significant Year" in your combined lives.

So when you were both at the ages of 7, 12, 19, 24, 31, 36, 43, etc., you were going through associated periods of important direction change in your life. For 8 out of these 12-month periods you were doing this together. Because my case history reveals that during these times people can feel somewhat out of control, or certainly out of their comfortable routine, the fact that this is happening to you both should promote greater feelings of empathy and understanding.

This is a simple matter of deductive reasoning. It is not based on any unproven linkage to some other cause. Like all of "Life Cycles Theory" it stands or falls on its case history evidence. Once again, I feel like I'm standing at the edge of a cliff, as I began to push forward with this brand new offshoot of the theory.

Returning to our basic premise, I'll now look at the next easy-to-understand example. In this case, let's say you and your partner were born in consecutive years rather than the same year, but that you were born in November of one year and that he/she was born in February of the next. For the actual 12 months total period you would share 9 months of "Confluence" or overlap. This would mean that you were even more "Confluent" by a month than the first couple.

It would, once again, suggest that you two had a high level of empathy and understanding and should first and foremost be really good friends, as well as lovers. I'm now going to illustrate these two scenarios and show exactly what I'm talking about with one of the world's best-known couples: the Duke and Duchess of Cambridge, William and Catherine. Catherine was born January 9, 1982, and William was born in the same year on June 21. This means they would share almost 7 months of "Confluence" for every "Significant Year" of their relationship.

They didn't meet until term one 2001, at St. Andrews University, so this is where our story begins. Since 2001 until the present, they are and have been a very compatible couple. We'll look at their biographical evidence in stages. If you are an amateur detective by nature, you might have noticed something interesting about when this was.

How old would they both have been during term one at St. Andrews in 2001? Yes, that's correct, they were both aged 19 and thus in their first adult, age 19 "Year of Broken Pathways". The premise during these years is that your pathway gets broken and your direction changes in an inexorable way, so that at the end of it things are never the same again.

They are said to have met in a bar close to the University and that when she was introduced to William Wales (as he was called then), Catherine became embarrassed and did a curtsey. William then got surprised and spilled his beer over himself.

A little comical and certainly not a case of meeting the smoky glance of a stranger across a crowded room and falling magnetically in love, however there is an obvious compatibility of personal styles. Following this somewhat awkward introduction, they became friends sharing student digs along with others and then sometime early in the next year, William (who was still in his age 19 "Year of Broken Pathways") bought a $300 front-row ticket for a charity fashion show that Catherine was modelling in.

She wore a revealing black see-through dress that has gone on to achieve fame in its own right. When she came down the catwalk, William was heard to exclaim, "Wow. Kate's hot!" This has been described by journalists as, "the dress that caught the Prince's eye and won his heart." Although they remained friends at this point, there was no doubt their mutual pathways were broken by their lives joining together.

This is a wonderful demonstration of "Confluence" in action. It is also a textbook description of how a "Year of Broken Pathways" is meant to unfold with its inexorable period of change.

Now we'll journey on to the period when they were both in their age 24, first adult "Year of Revolution". The key element we will be looking at here is the mutual period of upheaval and regeneration in their lives. Specifically, we will look at their combined seven months of "Confluence", which is the back half of the year 2006. What happened then? Well, this was the only time in their lives, before their marriage, when they broke up for a short period.

The split began when William was stationed at Dorset on a live-in basis and Catherine was in London. He was encouraged to be one of the boys and get out a bit at the surrounding pubs and clubs, where he met some of the local girls. These girls were not discrete and courted publicity, which must have been trying for Catherine. William also met some aristocratic girls, who caught his eye, but this was largely under the radar.

Still, Catherine put all this aside and was looking forward to attending William's passing out parade at Sandhurst in December 2006, which would have been her first high-profile event with the Queen in attendance. This, however, is not what happened at all. William announced that it was too soon for him to settle down and that they should split up.

This is the veritable definition of upheaval, both individually and in their combined lives. William was still in his age 24 "Year of Revolution" until June 2007, and there was much more to come for him. For a period of time, they led separate lives and during this time William stated that he had a life-altering experience, when he learned that a young female intelligence officer he had trained with was killed in Iraq. He said it made him think about his life and the things that matter.

This could also, doubtlessly, be traced to one single day when he learned this news. It was to be his own "Moment of Breakthrough" and he and Catherine were reconciled not too long after. This is a classic example of the potential for the effects of a "Year of Revolution" to be heightened even more when two people, who are in a relationship, undergo it together.

In the midst of their relationship turmoil, it is easy to forget the most straightforward correlation of the age of 24 and the ushering in of a new age/era in career terms. In William's case it is obvious. During this time he graduated from his military academy and became an army officer.

Now we'll move on for a period of seven years "Unbroken Forward Momentum" to their last combined "Significant Year", which was their combined age 31 "Year of Broken Pathways". This was the back half of the year 2013.

What significant event happened then to them as a couple? Any takers? I need to mention first, that their wedding had taken place two years previously, so it is not this, which is a good example of major events not all falling into the "Significant Years". It is rather the birth of their first child, Prince George, on July 22, 2013. As anyone who has gone through this milestone in their lives will know, things are forever changed when you become a family.

However following this, in September, which is right in the middle of the seven months period of "Confluence", came an official announcement that Prince William will be leaving the armed forces and the family will be moving from Anglesey in Wales to Kensington Palace in London.

This was to set in train a major lifestyle change for them both. In Catherine's case it meant an end to her relatively anonymous existence, in the idyllic setting of Anglesey, a pretty island off the Welsh coast. They had lived simply in a farmhouse, where Kate was seen shopping in the local supermarket and taking walks on the beach at Lupo. In her case it was never a truer example of your pathway gets broken and you can't return to where you had been.

In William's case it also meant big changes, as he had spent the last seven years in the structured world of the Army (an excellent example of the seven years of "Unbroken Forward Momentum") and now had to undergo a period of exploring just what his new direction might be. This was to be the uphill nature of his challenge that was not to be resolved in a hurry.

At the beginning of 2014 (while he was still aged 31), he undertook a ten-week bespoke course in Agricultural Management, because he would eventually inherit the Duchy of Cornwall from his father. Some students at Cambridge criticised his lower A levels and reduction in fees, saying he got in because of who he was.

More serious criticism surfaced a year later, when it was reported he had only spent 47 days on Royal duties. Currently we see William almost continuously in the news, because of his many engagements, so such remarks no longer apply; but it is acknowledged that he went through a learning phase. Kate also had a similar learning curve, as she slowly adapted to the pressure of being constantly in the public spotlight.

The theory of "Confluence" would say that for a couple undergoing these mutual challenges at the same time, it should promote empathy and understanding, and potentially great support. Their closeness as a couple when in the public eye bears testament to this. We have now completed an analysis of all their current adult "Significant Years", so it is time for me to unveil just how I would display this graphically for you.

What I am seeking to do is to summarise the shared biographic material during their periods of "Confluence" and show what it means in terms of their relationship. This is shown below and will form the basis of the first such teaching example. It is fitting, I feel, to use a contemporary case of such a well-known couple, because almost everyone has heard of them and they are featured almost constantly in the media.

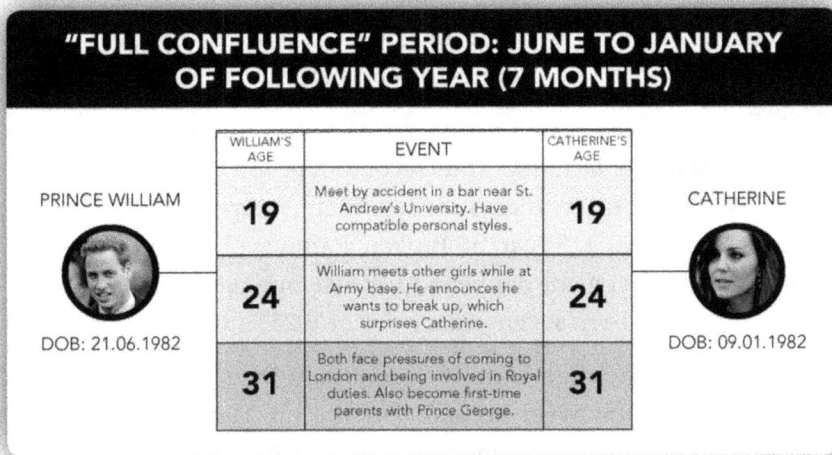

"FULL CONFLUENCE" PERIOD: JUNE TO JANUARY OF FOLLOWING YEAR (7 MONTHS)

	WILLIAM'S AGE	EVENT	CATHERINE'S AGE	
PRINCE WILLIAM DOB: 21.06.1982	19	Meet by accident in a bar near St. Andrew's University. Have compatible personal styles.	19	CATHERINE DOB: 09.01.1982
	24	William meets other girls while at Army base. He announces he wants to break up, which surprises Catherine.	24	
	31	Both face pressures of coming to London and being involved in Royal duties. Also become first-time parents with Prince George.	31	

The next similar type of "Confluence" occurs where a couple's ages are 12 years apart. So, if one partner is born in the year 1963 and the other is born in 1975, they would be "Confluent" for the amount of time in the year they share in common. Now I just happen to be describing the years of birth for arguably the world's most high-profile, ex-couple here. Any takers on this?

The answer is Brad Pitt, who was born December 18, 1963, and Angelina Jolie, who was born June 4, 1975. They would share almost seven months of "Confluence" for every "Significant Year" when they were a couple, which is just about identical to William and Catherine.

I have some more theory to unveil before I visit their analysis, so fans of the former couple will have to wait a little, but I do promise a no-holds-barred coverage. All other twelve-year age pairings will work for couples, even though some may include pieces of a year before or a year that follows. The last common one is a 24-year age gap, usually with the male being the older.

This example of "Confluence" just happens to fit another of the most celebrated couples in history. One was born December 25, 1899, (meaning his "Year of Revolution" covers most of the year 1900) and the other on September 16, 1924. This time it's Humphrey Bogart and Lauren Bacall, who shared around 3½ months of "Confluence" and they first met in one of those combined years just like William and Catherine.

All of the above instances of twelve-year groupings will be classified as "Full Confluence", because they cover every possible combined "Significant Year" of the history of a couple's relationship. Both parties are on parallel tracks, as it were, from the very beginning. It should promote understanding, empathy, and great support for all life's successes and struggles; but as you can patently see, in the case of Jolie-Pitt and others, it is not guaranteed to go the distance.

Now it is time to introduce the second type of "Confluence" that can occur. This is where one partner is in, say, their "Year of Revolution", whilst the other partner is in a "Year of Broken Pathways". In one very famous couple, such an arrangement happened because one person was born in 1932 and their partner was born seven years prior in 1925.

They would share the amount of overlapping time, in that year and for a portion of the next, for every second "Significant Year" in their lives as a couple (i.e., in their case when one was aged 36, the other would have been aged 43).

As you can see, this would be only half as much as it is for the cases of "Full Confluence". It would also mean they are never in a "Year of Revolution" together, which is the most fundamental time of upheaval and sudden, often unanticipated, change. The process during a "Year of Broken Pathways" tends to be more of an inexorable passage to a prolonged period of challenge, than a sudden storm ushering in a new era. For these reasons, I would deem it not as important to their lives in general.

In line with using straightforward terminology, I would call this second example "Partial Confluence". The question then becomes, "is there a difference between "Full Confluence" and "Partial Confluence" in terms of a couple's relationship?" In other words, what does the data tell us? This is an area I have explored in some detail and the short answer is yes, there is a difference.

Let me highlight this through the famous couple example I have just cited. It belongs to Richard Burton (born November 10, 1925) and Elizabeth Taylor (born February 27, 1932). They were "Confluent" for the period between November and February (i.e., for around 3½ months) for every second "Significant Year". You can see how this was only half of what William and Kate, or Brad and Angelina, had and also for only half the available times. So quite a bit less. The theory would say simply, that the stronger the "Confluence" a couple has, the better. Let's check out the reality of this.

Quite a number of sources attest, that when Richard Burton met Elizabeth Taylor on the set of *Cleopatra*, he was aged 36 and thus in his major midlife "Year of Revolution". He clearly saw her as just another notch on his belt, boasting to colleagues beforehand, that he was going to have sex with the 29-year-old English star, "I just need two days with her. It's guaranteed." This was to mark the beginning of one of the greatest celebrity tempestuous relationships ever recorded. Most certainly not what Burton expected.

The fighting and break-ups began almost immediately and Burton didn't leave his long-suffering first wife for quite a while. It also caused a massive scandal when Taylor left Eddie Fisher to be with the then-married Burton. When they eventually both divorced their partners in April, 1963, Liz was just at the beginning of her age 31 "Year of Broken Pathways". This also meant Burton was aged 37 at the same time and in these two instances (first meeting and divorce), or their subsequent 1964 marriage, there was no period of "Confluence".

For Liz, this "Year of Broken Pathways" also meant the challenge of coping with the negative reviews and massive cost overruns that plagued *Cleopatra*. Though the movie grossed $26 million, it also bankrupted Fox Studios, who sued the couple for damaging its prospects with their behaviour. After marriage, Liz's pathway was changed and she largely only made movies with Richard.

The most famous was *Who's Afraid Of Virginia Woolf*. It was said this movie mirrored their own warring marriage, which included physicality and hurling objects, particularly when they were drunk. The only time in their relationship when there was a brief period of "Confluence" was from November, 1968 to February, 1969. What, if anything, happened then? This period is marked by Liz receiving news of her father's death in November, 1968, and being inconsolable with grief.

This whole episode though, must be put into the broader perspective of Liz's age 36 "Year of Revolution" (February, 1968 to February. 1969). Earlier in the year, in May, Richard bought Liz a very large diamond ring known as the Krupp Diamond. She so adored this ring that she wore it almost every day for the rest of her life.

After her death it was called the Elizabeth Taylor Diamond and as such, could be considered the highest tangible expression of Richard's affections, along with his quote from around the same time, "I have been inordinately lucky all my life but the greatest luck of all has been Elizabeth."

Extracts from their personal diaries reveal that at 36 a catastrophe befell the Burtons. Elizabeth was forced to undergo a hysterectomy in July, 1968, ending any hope of them having their own child. Also in June, 1968, Ifor Jenkins (Richard's elder brother, whom he idolised) was paralysed from the neck down after a heavy drinking session together. This was the subject of a controversial film *The Secret*, which claimed Richard may have pushed Ifor during an argument, leading him to henceforth lead a life of self-destructive guilt. Come what may, Richard's age 43 "Year of Broken Pathways" was all about facing his demons, including being told that unless he gave up the booze he would be dead in a couple of years.

So Liz, at 36, did not have any great breakthroughs or achievements (in fact quite the reverse) and though unusual, I sometimes find this type of data, particularly where the individual has had one or more exceptional earlier "Years of Revolution".

In the case of Liz, her career began as a child actress, winning fame in her age 12 "Year of Revolution" with *National Velvet* and in her age 24 "Year of Revolution" with the movie *Giant*, which was her first substantial dramatic success and led to her golden age as a celebrated leading actress.

During her age 36 year, her movie career waned considerably with a couple of flops and it ushered in a new era of doing a limited number of theatrical films, along with some TV appearances. It could be said this really marked the end of her golden age.

History attests, that for all the protestations of eternal love between her and Richard in 1968, they did not last for long or save their tempestuous marriage. They divorced in June, 1974, which happened during Richard's age 48 "Year of Revolution", so this 12-year cycle for him (i.e., from age 36 to age 48) was marked by the beginning and close of his relationship with Liz.

A subsequent reconciliation, a short time later, only led to a very short-lived second marriage, a bit like Muhammad Ali's ill-fated final fights. No, there is nothing on display here, over a period of time, that marks them as a well-settled couple, who are each other's best friends as well as lovers.

Other famous couples with "Partial Confluence" have had their troubles and break-ups and the weight of evidence seems to strongly support "Full Confluence" as being the best for long term success. Before I close this introduction to the theory of "Confluence", I want to add a couple more easy-to-understand terms.

The first refers to the sometimes narrow period of time a couple shares "Confluence" for in their relationship. Because these can be pivotal moments, where things can go one way or the other, I call them "Windows of Opportunity".

I will analyse some cases where things turn out well and also where they do not. For instance, let's imagine the worst for a brief moment in the case of William and Catherine. During their short period of break-up, they could have found themselves attracted to others, to the extent that a reconciliation didn't happen.

The second of my concepts refers to periods of time generally, when people are living through one of their "Significant Years". So if you are reading this now and you are aged say 24, 31, or 36, you are meant to be experiencing a period of important change in your life. I use the phrase you are in "Real Time", because you could notice the feeling of things being somewhat out of control.

To both undergo important and sometimes dramatic change and be aware of it at the same time will heighten the experience still more. For a startling example of what I am talking about please see Chapter 9 of *The Life Cycles Revolution*, where I describe in great detail my own "Years of Revolution".

This has particular application to people either in or beginning a relationship. Since their "Window of Opportunity" can be small, they can be said to be in "Real Time Confluence", if they are aware of what it means. As an example, neither William nor Catherine (who met in their "Window of Opportunity" at age 19) had any idea of this when they first got introduced, but if they had, they might have noted an attraction that seemed almost fated to be.

These life-changing meetings happening in a time of mutual direction change and upheaval deserves, I believe, to lay claim to being called a "Fated Relationship". In no way does this suggest that other love matches and life-long grand passions cannot occur outside this narrow framework, but my research will concentrate on well-publicised cases where it does.

There are many suitable and compatible long-term relationships, which have no "Confluence" whatsoever and that unless there is a spark of chemistry between a couple, then the period of "Confluence" alone can't light the fire.

So, as I stated at the outset, this is not a panacea for how to find true love or a guarantee of success. It's more complex than that and your skepticism about it can be forgiven. All I ask is that you examine my biographical evidence to gain a greater understanding and be your own judge, as you learn to apply it to your life. It will forever alter the way you view all your many relationships.

Since I have introduced quite a few new terms, which will constitute all of the additional theory, it is appropriate to review these now.

1. "Confluence"- An overlap of the "Significant Years" shared by two or more individuals in some form of relationship. It is meant to promote greater empathy and understanding.

2. "Full Confluence"- Where a couple are born in the same 12-month period or any 12-year multiples. They thus share time in every single "Significant Year" of their relationship.

3. "Partial Confluence"- Where a couple share a mix of "Significant Years" for every second such occurrence. This is said to be of lesser influence generally.

4. "Window of Opportunity"- The period when couples are both sharing "Confluence".

5. "Real Time"- To be aware of the experience of undergoing changes in

a "Significant Year".

6. "Real Time Confluence"- To be aware of the experience of meeting a potential partner (or other important life event), when you are both in a period of "Confluence".

7. "Fated Relationship"- For a couple to meet in a period of "Confluence".

CHAPTER FOUR

FAMOUS COUPLES AND CONFLUENCE

The best way to illustrate a new idea about people's lives is to show what it means in cases most of us have heard of. After all, if I stuck to examples, who are without a significant public profile, I could rightfully be suspected of doctoring my evidence. This is because there would be no easy way to verify what I have stated. If I also maintained that some unprovable link to an occult idea caused my results, I would similarly become no better than every other discredited theory.

But, if I can show how my independent, evidence-driven theory of "Confluence" works with a wide variety of household name celebrities, it will provide a strong platform for discussion and further proof of the validity of the whole "Life Cycles Theory".

So, without further ado, let's begin with JFK and Jackie. John Fitzgerald Kennedy was born May 29, 1917, and Jacqueline Bouvier was born July 28, 1929. This means that for every combined "Significant Year", they shared an amazing 10 out of a possible 12 months of "Confluence".

What was the story of how they met? In a forgotten corner of her correspondence, Jackie wrote a note to a Newport friend, that in early 1949, she had just met Jack Kennedy on a train journey. This was in their combined "Years of Broken Pathway" (at 19/31).

It was the same age for her, as when William and Catherine met, only this time the protagonists are separated by 12 years. So, if you will, they also met in "Real Time Confluence" (although they wouldn't have had any idea about it) and thus this marks them as a "Fated Relationship".

Her description of him was, "a charming, confident and handsome but insistent flirt, to whom she responded with indifferent amusement, yet absolute attraction." As a blueprint for their marriage it was very close. As a description of a fated relationship, it is spot on. You don't actually know why the attraction happens, it just happens.

From this fleeting first meeting their lives took different directions for the next several years; he to a seat in Congress and she to completing her Bachelor of Arts degree. However, most standard biographical summaries first mention a meeting in 1952 at a dinner party. This reunion was close, but not quite, to their next shared "Significant Year", when they would have been aged 24 and 36, which was the period July, 1953 to May, 1954. What major event happened in their shared lives then?

The answer is their wedding held in September, 1953. It was the society wedding of the year. It is instructive to hear Jack Kennedy's quote of his wife Jackie, "I'd known a lot of attractive women in my lifetime...but of them all there was only one I could have married...and I married her." There is certainly a "meant to be" element here, isn't there?

As well as the romance aspect of "Confluence", we also have the friendship and empathy side. One serves to reinforce the other. During the early days of their marriage, Jack had to undergo two potentially life threatening back operations, which were a result of a war injury. This amounted to their combined "Moments of Setback/Frustration", that usually precedes the "Moment of Breakthrough", which in their case was a successful outcome for both operations.

It must be acknowledged that JFK's philandering took a great emotional toll on Jackie over the next period, so this "Fated Relationship" was not exactly a bed of roses. A poignant quote about this is, "Jackie was a woman full of love and full of hurt. They were two private people, two cocoons married to each other, trying to reach into each other. I think that she felt that he, being so much older than her, that it was up to him to reach more. But he couldn't."

However, things were about to change for the better during their next combined period of "Confluence", when they would be in their respective ages 43/31 "Years of Broken Pathways". This corresponded to the time July, 1960 to May, 1961. There are no prizes for guessing here, that Jack's seven-year career as a Senator was about to be forever changed by the 1960 Presidential Election.

This is an axiomatic example of the principle of seven years of "Unbroken Forward Momentum" being forever altered during a "Year of Broken Pathways". However, in addition, both he and 31-year-old Jackie faced this enormous challenge together.

Jackie, even though pregnant, helped in the campaign and her knowledge of languages was quite beneficial. It was a narrow victory and she was one of the youngest First Ladies. It has been written of this time that, "they fell in love all over again," as they had to face both the campaign and gaining respect in the top job. It was said after a year in the White House, "the dynamic of their relationship was changing and there was a more consistent pattern of expression of mutual love and devotion." There was also no doubt that Jack needed her comfort and advice, especially around the time of the Bay of Pigs crisis.

So their relationship took a much more positive turn and again their mutual support and empathy were on full display. Indeed there is no better way to sum things up than Jackie's quote from the Cuban Missile crisis of 1962.

"If anything happens, we're all going to stay right here with you," she remembers telling her husband. "Even if there's not room in the bomb shelter in the White House. ... I just want to be with you, and I want to die with you, and the children do, too – than live without you."

This is now displayed graphically for you.

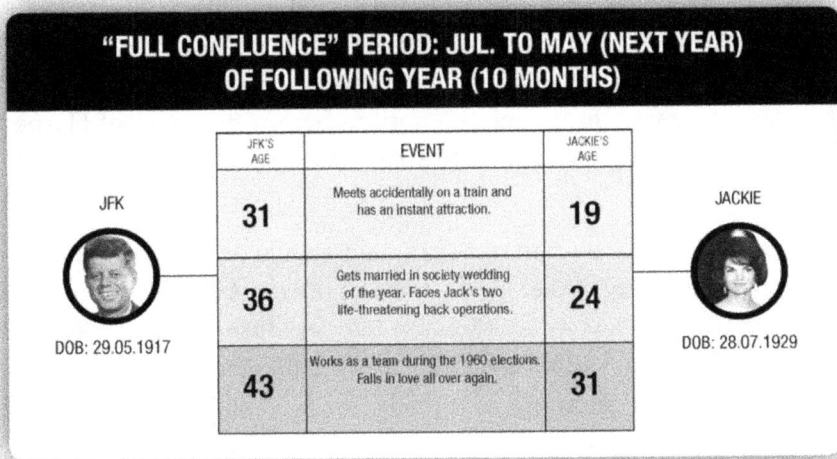

"FULL CONFLUENCE" PERIOD: JUL. TO MAY (NEXT YEAR) OF FOLLOWING YEAR (10 MONTHS)

JFK	JFK'S AGE	EVENT	JACKIE'S AGE	JACKIE
JFK	31	Meets accidentally on a train and has an instant attraction.	19	JACKIE
DOB: 29.05.1917	36	Gets married in society wedding of the year. Faces Jack's two life-threatening back operations.	24	DOB: 28.07.1929
	43	Works as a team during the 1960 elections. Falls in love all over again.	31	

Now we'll visit another of the great public romances of the modern age - Humphrey Bogart and Lauren Bacall. Humphrey was born December 25, 1899, and Lauren was born Betty Joan Perske on September 16, 1924. This means that from the period September 16 to December 25, they would share about 3½ months of "Confluence" for every combined "Significant Year".

There is no doubt that they were the loves of each other's lives, but because of the 24-year age gap, Bogart had a lot more experience in the world of romance and marriage. He began his career on the stage in Broadway. His personal life included three early and unhappy marriages and many brief affairs, mostly with actresses. One biography claimed he slept with around 1,000 women including Bette Davis, Jean Harlow, Marlene Dietrich, and Ingrid Bergman. That's considerably more than the average, but it would be fair to say that the essential spark that ignites lovers at a deeper personal level, had not yet been lit.

Then we see the entry into his life of a 19-year-old inexperienced actress named Lauren Bacall, when she was auditioning for a part in *To Have And Have Not*. This was also a time in which he would have been in his age 43 "Year of Broken Pathways", so we are dealing with their first available adult period of "Confluence". Same as for William and Catherine, and JFK and Jackie.

It was thus a "Window of Opportunity" and it was to become a "Fated Relationship" in terms of the theory. Now let's have a look at their separate lives in this "Year of Broken Pathways", which is a time of challenge and direction change.

We'll take the then, Betty Bacall, first. When she was 19, the wife of independent film director Howard Hawks (whose nickname was 'Slim', the name of Bacall's character in the movie) noticed her on the cover of Harper's Bazaar. She showed the photo to her husband, who soon signed her for the role.

He changed her name to Lauren Bacall, and changed her style and voice; adopting a lower, sexier tone, that made it one of the most distinctive voices in Hollywood. During screen tests, to minimise her nervousness, she pressed her chin against her chest and tilted her eyes upward. This created 'The Look', which became Bacall's trademark.

On its own this is highly relevant evidence for fateful direction change in her "Year of Broken Pathways" (no different to the making of Edith Piaf, or the making of Lady Gaga, at exactly the same age, both of which I've previously featured).

However, Humphrey Bogart had his own dramas during his "Year of Broken Pathways" at 43. His third marriage to Mayo Methot had been a disaster, while their alcoholism and fighting, including gunplay, were legendary. They were known as the 'battling Bogarts', she was called 'Sluggy' and their home (the scene of much of their fighting, including stabbing Bogart in the shoulder) was known as 'Sluggy Hollow'.

He was ready for a change and wanted peace, not war. This was fertile ground to be introduced to a nice Jewish girl, 24 years his junior and not a big drinker. It was said that Bogart fell in love with the role of 'Slim', played by Bacall, and that he wanted her to always play this role for him. But whatever the idiosyncrasies were, their relationship worked until his death in 1957.

So, this shows exactly how a combined "Year of Broken Pathways" can work, as two completely different lives meet in a time of "Confluence". Of passing interest here, is that at 36, when Bogart was in his important midlife "Year of Revolution", he had his acknowledged breakthrough role in *The Petrified Forest*. His acting was called brilliant, compelling and superb.

Continuing on the Hollywood theme, we'll next examine a rarer example of a 36-year difference in ages of a famous couple. Since a person's age 36 year features so prominently in "Life Cycles Theory", it will be interesting if this age gap has any extra connection. The iconic Charlie Chaplin was born April 16, 1889, and his fourth and final wife, Oona O'Neill, was born May 14, 1925, so they shared an amazing 11 out of a possible 12 months of "Confluence", for each of their combined "Significant Years". This is the most yet studied.

Up until they met, in early 1943, it was said in a biography by Peter Ackroyd that,

> *"Chaplin's love life had been a complete mess for all his fame and fortune."*

There was an absolute hoard of women willing to accept his advances (he boasted of sleeping with around 2,000 females and showed a preference for actresses who were under 18), but Ackroyd stated he never really liked women and it stemmed from an unhappy childhood, after being abandoned by his mother at the age of 7. At that stage there would seem little prospect of 53-year-old Chaplin changing his wicked ways. After all, why should another young 17-year-old would-be actress, named Oona O'Neill, prove any different to so many others?

History will show, that against all odds, she did the unthinkable and that is to remain married to Chaplin until his death at the age of 88. She also bore him 8 of his 11 children, and provided the only settled family existence and lasting happiness he ever knew. When they married soon after meeting, this young aspiring actress was just a month past her eighteenth birthday.

However, she immediately gave away her career and became a housewife, saying she was, "happy to stay in the background". Although, in line with the mutual support aspect of "Confluence", she also spent time in the studios if Chaplin was working and he often sought her opinion.

She stood in for lead actress Claire Bloom in the movie *Limelight* (1952), when Bloom wasn't available. They faced the dramas of Chaplin being called a communist, having his US re-entry permit denied and relocating to Switzerland, together as a couple, and were thus a true partnership.

This successful example of "Confluence" is perhaps the greatest showcase for my unusual ideas. Once again this extremely rare 36-year age difference, provides an equally rare love story for the ages. He described meeting Oona as, "the happiest event of my life" and claimed to have found perfect love. She, in turn, is said to have worshipped him.

Also of note is the obvious match of Chaplin's career to his two prominent younger "Years of Revolution" (at ages 24 and 36). When he was aged 24, he began his career in films after signing a contract with Keystone Studios and releasing his first film. At 36, he released the movie *The Gold Rush*, which became one of the highest grossing movies of the silent era, making $5 million. Chaplin felt it was the best movie he had made to this point and, "...the picture I want to be remembered by" (not unlike Napoleon's comments after his most famous victory at 36).

Switching to another very prominent Hollywood love story, we'll now examine the long relationship between Spencer Tracy and Katharine Hepburn. I have unearthed so much relevant material here, it seems to cross the boundaries I have drawn for subsequent chapters on the themes of friendship and family. I will cover most, but not all, at this point, for my last example is truly stunning.

Spencer Tracy was born April 5, 1900, and Katherine Hepburn was born May 12, 1907. This means that there was some 7 years difference in their ages, which correlates with "Partial Confluence" for every second "Significant Year" of their combined lives. However, though this is less than for other cases, it did amount to 11 out of a possible 12 months (like Chaplin and O'Neill, but for only half as many years).

Though Tracy had a string of affairs with leading actresses, it was only Hepburn who gets mentioned in personal summaries, because of the length (26 years) and intensity of their famous relationship. They didn't meet in a period of "Confluence", however there was a remarkable reaction by

Hepburn, who said, "I knew right away that I found him irresistible." Her strongly independent streak also evaporated when she was with him, and she was said to have mothered and obeyed him.

Tracy opposed getting a divorce on both religious and family grounds, particularly over guilt feelings towards his deaf son. They thus concealed their relationship and lived separately until his final years.

In fact, the best example of a period of "Confluence" for them, was the final period leading up to Tracy's death in June, 1967. They were ages 67 and 60 respectively and he was in a "Year of Broken Pathways" while she was in a "Year of Revolution". He died in her arms, but when it came to the funeral she respected the wishes of his wife Louise and did not attend.

Instead, she followed the hearse until it got to the chapel and then left saying to herself, "goodbye friend, here's where I leave you." This is a most evocative illustration of their relationship.

In career terms again, his midlife age 36 "Year of Revolution", features his breakthrough role in the movie *Fury*. It was said that, "audiences, who just a year ago had no clear handle on him, were suddenly turning out to see him. It was a transition that was nothing short of miraculous…".

Of course, I would say it was just one more in an absolute avalanche of miracles and near-miracles at 36, that I have unearthed. As a preview to a forthcoming chapter, I'll show an example of "Confluence" in friendship terms. There is quite a "Confluence" connection between Tracy and Hepburn, and our previous Hollywood couple, Bogart and Bacall.

You might not have remembered but Bogie and Spencer's birthdays were very close and they shared around 9 months of "Confluence" for every combined "Significant Year". This made them the best of friends and both couples were very close as well.

They were thrown together in the early part of their careers with the making of the movie *Up The River* in 1930, where they became good friends and drinking buddies. It was Tracy who gave him the nickname of Bogie. In their combined age 36 "Years of Revolution" they first made their names in the big league. In fact, if they were alive today, it would have been called a bromance.

Both couples hit it off and got involved jointly with the making of *The African Queen* (1951), starring Bogie and Hepburn. They also shared a similarity in their clandestine relationships (at least in the early days of Bogie and Bacall). This is a wonderful example of all the possible interconnections where "Confluence" was present.

I'm going to switch away from tinsel town now and cover one of the greatest acknowledged love stories from the nineteenth century - Victoria and Albert. So much has been written and anyone who knows a bit about history would have heard of them. They would easily make a 'Top 10 Famous Couples of All Time' list. As I was writing this, I noticed a very popular TV miniseries on their lives was screening, bringing them to the fore of public consciousness once again.

The future Queen Victoria was born May 24, 1819, and the future Prince Albert was born August 26, 1819, meaning they were born in the same year and thus shared an impressive 9 months out of a possible 12 for "Confluence" in every shared "Significant Year". This is even stronger than William and Catherine, and is only eclipsed by Chaplin and O'Neill.

Their first chaperoned meeting at age 17 confirmed Victoria's attraction. She wrote, "he (Albert) is extremely handsome...he possesses every quality that could be desired to render me extremely happy." No question, she was smitten from the get go, which happened with virtually all the others we have discussed.

They married at age 20, so their first period of "Confluence" would have been when they were both in their age 24 "Year of Revolution", which is the period August, 1843 to May, 1844. What events happened at this time? There weren't any standout historical moments, but there were a couple of foreign relations issues in Ireland and France, and the latter involved Prince Albert as well.

The couple visited the French King, Louis Philippe in September, 1843, and relations were very cordial between the two, the families being connected by marriage. She was the first English monarch to visit France since Henry VIII. Later on, though, there was an incident in early 1844, in the newly French-controlled Tahiti.

This involved maltreatment of a British Consul, George Pritchard, and it caused a wave of unrest in England, which the Queen and her government feared at one time must end in war. This was doubtlessly their combined "Moment of Setback/Frustration" and its peaceful resolution would have been their combined "Moment of Breakthrough".

When they were both in their age 31 "Year of Broken Pathways", in the period August, 1850 to May, 1851, there was a personal highlight for Albert, with the opening of the famous Great Exhibition of Science and Industry. Albert was President of the Society of Arts and fought hard to get each stage of the costly venture approved. It was opened by Victoria in early May, 1851, in the Crystal Palace, a specially designed glass building.

It proved a great success, generating a surplus of 180,000 pounds, which was used to establish the Natural History Museum, Science Museum, and Royal Albert Hall. It was said in one biography that, "for both the Queen and Prince Consort the highlight of their reign came with the opening of the Great Exhibition." Victoria said, "I do feel proud at the thought of what my beloved Albert's great mind has conceived." Once again this is evidence of a strong bond of partnership during a period of "Confluence".

Albert, in particular, had managed to turn initial skepticism, about his own background and fitness to rule, into a wave of success. Unfortunately, life does not run in a straight line and we'll now discuss arguably the greatest challenge faced by Victoria and Albert, and what was done to come out on top. It is no surprise that this should coincide with the period in which they were both in their all important age 36 "Year of Revolution" (August, 1855 to May, 1856).

This is squarely in the latter period of the very long and damaging Crimean War. At the outset of the war, both Victoria and Albert were very unpopular while Albert, quite unjustly, was accused of trying to influence the government on behalf of Russia. This came about because of his German background and their family links to the Russian Royals.

There is mention of these baseless rumours still being in existence in the first half of 1855. Victoria, for her part, had regained much popularity by showing consistent support for the Army and had personally supervised committees of relief for the wounded. She had seconded the efforts of Florence Nightingale and visited the wounded in hospital.

In September, 1855, Sebastopol fell, after a siege of nearly a year and this brought an honourable peace well within sight. However, not too long after this both the Queen and the Prince received heavy criticism again, when the betrothal of their daughter to the eldest son of the Prince of Prussia was announced. *The Times* on October 3 denounced it as, "truckling to a paltry German Dynasty".

It didn't help relations with the French either. Here is their joint "Moment of Frustration/Setback" in their combined "Years of Revolution", that is in line with the theory. You can plainly see that only the very famous would have sufficient year by year, and in this case month by month, commentary to allow this type of analysis. So what was to be their combined "Moment of Breakthrough"?

The Queen, as just stated, had a strong interest in Army affairs and one of her chief areas of concern was in awards and medals. It was at the insistence of Albert, that the Queen instituted the Victoria Cross, as the highest award for gallantry in January, 1856. It was to become the most prestigious of all British Awards, with the first recipients granted at the end of the Crimean War.

It became very popular and could reasonably be called their greatest lasting mutual legacy. No question about it, this was their combined "Moment of Breakthrough". Again, a summary of these highlights is now shown.

"FULL CONFLUENCE" PERIOD: AUG. TO MAY (NEXT YEAR) OF FOLLOWING YEAR (9 MONTHS)

VICTORIA	VICTORIA'S AGE	EVENT	ALBERT'S AGE	ALBERT
DOB: 24.05.1819	24	Faces foreign relations issue with France, that could have led on to war.	24	DOB: 26.08.1819
	31	Victoria opens the Great Exhibition of science and industry, which was the work of Albert.	31	
	36	They overcome criticism of their daughter marrying a Prussian Prince by initiating the Victoria Cross.	36	

Some stories, like this one, are so good I can hardly believe it. You see, I wrote this passage as I did the analysis. I had no prior knowledge, so for me it was a true 'blind test'. We'll leave the happy Royal Couple for now and switch both continents and centuries to cover another one of the acknowledged greatest public love affairs of all time, Juan and Eva (Evita) Peron.

The name Eva Peron is very widely known, thanks to the musical and the movie that bears her name. Her rise to fame from the humble beginnings of an illegitimate birth in rural Argentina, combined with her trade union activities to better the conditions for the working poor, made her a true national icon.

She came to be called the 'Spiritual Leader of The Nation'.

We are most concerned, however, about her relationship with her much older politician husband, Juan Peron, and whether there was any "Confluence" present. Eva Maria Duarte was born May 7, 1919, and Juan Domingo Peron was born October 8, 1895.

This means they were another rare example of a 24-year age gap and they shared 7 months of "Confluence" between October and May for every single combined "Significant Year". Since they didn't meet until she was a young adult and she died at the age of 33, there isn't a large window to work with.

Eva had escaped her impoverished early life and became a successful actress in Buenos Aires in her early 20's. She was in her age 24, first adult, "Year of Revolution" (May, 1943 to May, 1944), when she first met 48-year-old Secretary of Labour, Juan Peron in January, 1944. They thus met in "Real Time Confluence", which marked them as a "Fated Relationship". This high-profile example demonstrates every element of "Life Cycles - Relationships" theory. So perfect, it is textbook.

Following an earthquake in San Juan, Argentina, killing some 10,000 people, Peron wished to have an artistic festival as a fundraiser, and invited radio and film actors to participate. At a gala, a week later, Juan met Eva and it was said, "she charmed him and they fell madly in love."

She referred to their meeting as her, "marvellous day" i.e., in effect describing her own "One Day Phenomenon". She promptly became his mistress and when they married in 1945, they went on to change the Argentinian political landscape entirely. They became one of the most beloved political couples of the era.

The last possible period of "Confluence" was when they were in their ages 31 and 55 "Years of Broken Pathway" respectively (i.e., October, 1950 to May, 1951). This featured Eva's health issues and her ultimate political ambitions. Because she had championed voting rights for women and founded the Female Peronist Party, she had set her sights on nomination for the 1951 elections as Vice President. However, the military leaders despised her and could not abide the thought, that she could succeed as President should Juan die.

As this fomented along, she eventually decided to publicly announce later that year, in August, that she would not run for office. The strength of her support from the unions and Peronist Women's Party is said to have surprised her husband, as he realised she was more popular than him. All the while, however, a second issue to do with Eva's health was intensifying. She had a number of incidents of fainting in public during 1950/1.

She, in fact, had an aggressive form of cervical cancer, although Juan kept this diagnosis from her. Eva knew her health was declining and this also convinced her that a bid for the Vice Presidency was not possible. You can see that, as a couple, they both faced the inexorable period of change and challenge, which the theory highlights for a "Year of Broken Pathways".

Now I'll examine a final very famous and unlikely couple, the well-known Marilyn Monroe and her second husband, the sporting legend, Joe DiMaggio. They had a brief and disastrous marriage, but in spite of this and Marilyn's promiscuity, there was a reasonable case for saying they were actually the loves of each other's lives.

Joseph Paul DiMaggio was born November 25, 1914, and Norma Jean Mortenson was born June 1, 1926. This meant they had 7 months of "Confluence" for each shared "Significant Year". He was a legendary baseball hero, who had just been forced into retirement by injuries and poor form in his age 36 "Year of Revolution". This ushered in his new age, whether he liked it or not.

She, on the other hand, was an up-and-coming actress in her age 24 "Year of Revolution", who had just signed a seven-year contract with Twentieth Century Fox, after successes in the films *All About Eve* and *The Asphalt Jungle*. She was now a recognised Hollywood star, which was her new age/direction.

Can you see the issue here? Their new eras had them going in opposite directions. They met in the next year after this, which took place in a restaurant in March, 1952. She was two hours late and Joe hardly spoke at all. Still, there was a spark and no denying his charisma. He managed, simply by being there, to command the whole room. They drove around for a couple of hours after this, finding each other fascinating. This perfectly describes the magic that can come when opposites, who have a strong level of "Confluence", get together.

Joe wanted her to give up acting and become his wife in a traditional sense and Marilyn's friends advised her against this union. He was also jealous because the attention she got was what he was used to getting. This was to become a short ride and a not so merry one when they decided to marry.

He was advised by a friend, who was a Hollywood agent, to accept her career as being like his former career, when he was on top. However, he could not control his jealousy and quite a few accounts talk of him beating her. He said she brought out the worst in him. It all came unstuck when he beat her up in their hotel room, after seeing the filming of the sexy skirt-flying shoot for *The Seven Year Itch*.

She received an uncontested divorce on the grounds of mental cruelty. She went to live with her then friend, Frank Sinatra, who was separated from his wife, Ava Gardner. That really should have been it, pure and simple. This union was a big mistake.

But Joe, according to biographers, never stopped loving Marilyn and went on to become her close friend and ally, genuinely caring for her welfare. He spent time in therapy himself and came back into her life with the unwinding of her marriage to Arthur Miller. This is the friendship side of "Confluence", as discussed in previous examples.

After leaving Miller, Marilyn took up again with Sinatra, who undoubtedly was in love with her. However, she was now in a self-destructive phase, taking a variety of drugs and alcohol, and ended up being admitted to the Payne Whitney Psychiatric Clinic. Unable to check herself out, she called her friend DiMaggio. Others did not help, but he did and interestingly claimed her as his wife.

During 1961 their relationship continued to grow and they enjoyed looking after each other. Her quote was, "to know Joe is there is like having a lifeguard." When she was advised to buy a home and her finances weren't good, it was Joe who loaned her $10,000 for her place in Brentwood.

However, she was also promiscuous during this time and when he was travelling with his job, she fell back in with Sinatra and the Kennedys. Joe was enraged when he saw her sing at Kennedy's birthday on May 19, 1962.

We now enter her tumultuous and brief age 36 "Year of Revolution" on June 1, which can see a major transformation in so many, many different lives. Following an argument after Kennedy's birthday, they then reconciled and she admitted to Joe that he had been right about so many things. This marked the beginning of her wisdom. He flew from New York to Los Angeles four times in July to be with her and quit his job that had meant constant travel. Quite a few different sources said they were going to remarry. I'll quote from DiMaggio's niece, June,

"They had planned to remarry on the day that turned out to be her funeral. She had a dress and had picked out her china dishes. Joe had a ring for her and there was talk they might adopt a child. If she was remarrying Joe, the love of her life, is she going to take her own life four days before?"

This transcendent moment of remarriage never happened, but ironically she knew who loved her the most and who was the true love of her life. Joe honoured his earlier promise, given during their first relationship, to ensure fresh flowers were placed on her grave three times a week for the next twenty years. He never remarried and would not allow friends or associates to utter the names of Sinatra, the Rat Pack or the Kennedys in his presence.

For a man with a difficult personality, who had fall-outs with his own family and many past friends, he gave of his very best for Marilyn. For a woman, who was so conflicted and capricious, who told Joe in February, 1962, that she was buying furniture in Mexico and returned with a handsome young Mexican screenwriter instead, she finally managed to reach her deepest emotional level with him.

Together they may have had a great life the second time around. This is the power of "Confluence", that sometimes makes the impossible, possible. They tragically were never together for any of their past periods of "Confluence" and their next period would have begun in late November, 1962, when Joe turned 48. Their best story, unfortunately, lies unwritten.

There is possibly no more poignant example of "Confluence" than this. It should coincidentally be mentioned that Marilyn shared no "Confluence" with either of her other two husbands or her serious relationship with Frank Sinatra, or the infamous 1962 fling with JFK (which caused Jackie so much grief). I have just combed through a list of 20 or so short relationships that she is rumoured to have had, and could not find any obvious matches there either.

This now completes a walk-through list of famous couples throughout different eras. Though it is not truly comprehensive, it does include many of the relationships mentioned in various lists. To summarise, we have now explored how the theory of "Confluence" operates in the lives of :

1. Prince William and Catherine (the only still-living example)

2. Richard Burton and Elizabeth Taylor (the scandal-ridden couple, who did not stay together and shared only a small amount of "Partial

Confluence")

3. John F. Kennedy and Jackie

4. Humphrey Bogart and Lauren Bacall

5. Charlie Chaplin and Oona O'Neill (not as well-known, but a very significant example in terms of their "Confluence")

6. Spencer Tracy and Katharine Hepburn (albeit a long-standing affair that lasted until Tracy's death)

7. Prince Albert and Queen Victoria

8. Juan and Eva Peron

9. Marilyn Monroe and Joe DiMaggio (the most tragic example)

The question I want to ask here is, "if I made this into a reasonably comprehensive all-time list, who might I add and have I analysed them before?"

The first couple that springs to mind is Marc Antony and Cleopatra. This is the ancient world's best example of a power couple and yes, I have analysed their lives. Cleopatra's date of birth is confirmed from a number of sources as October, 69 BC, and so this well-known couple did not share any period of "Confluence".

However, their lives were both very closely intertwined with that of the renowned Julius Caesar, with whom both share a degree of "Confluence". In Mark Antony's case it was 6 months of "Partial Confluence" for every second "Significant Year". Julius Caesar was born July 13, 100 BC, and Antony was born January 14, 83 BC. In Cleopatra's case it was 10 months of "Partial Confluence", but in different "Significant Years" to Antony.

A good example of this in practice is Cleopatra's age 24 "Year of Revolution" (i.e., when Julius Caesar would have been in his age 55 "Year of Broken Pathways"). This was the period in which he was murdered in the Senate. She had borne him a son called Caesarion and was living with him in Rome. The fact that Caesar planned to marry her outraged the conservative Republicans, as it broke the laws against bigamy and marrying foreigners. She was seen as a dangerous seductress.

The 1963 movie shows a scene the day before his death when Caesar wanted absolute control as Emperor, which would have given Cleopatra everything she desired. However, in one fateful day, it was all brought undone and she had to flee Rome instead. This was her personal new age and the very definition of what a "Year of Revolution" can stand for.

Following Caesar's death, she forged a new relationship with his formerly extremely loyal general, Marc Antony, and also bore him a son and heir, potentially to some or all of the Roman Empire. You can see, that in equal measure, she had an attraction to power as well as love in these two relationships. Her prime goal was the continuation of her Ptolemaic Dynasty.

When she was in her age 36 "Year of Revolution" (October, 33 BC to October, 32 BC), Cleopatra issued a coin with Antony's portrait on one side and hers on the other. The inscription read, "Queen of Kings and her sons who are Kings". This, combined with Antony's intention to establish a second Senate in Alexandra, was the perfect moment to get an inquiry started to strip Antony of his power.

Octavian (Caesar's adopted son and ruler of the Western Roman Empire) illegally seized Antony's will. The Senate apparently was not moved by making Caesarion, Caesar's legal heir, or leaving his estate to Cleopatra's children; but it was Antony's desire to be buried alongside her in Alexandria that outraged them. The Senate declared war on Cleopatra, which of course meant Antony as well. This was her fateful turning point. It was to directly lead to the Battle of Actium and the demise of both her and Marc Antony. This second split with Rome was similar in nature to what had happened to her at 24 when she was once again so tantalisingly close to fulfilling her lifetime ambition, but it was all taken from her in one day.

Moving through history, we will now visit another of the all-time famous (or in this case infamous) couples, Henry VIII and Anne Boleyn. They also did not share any "Confluence", but it has been well established that Anne had a strong attraction to power, even at the cost of a split with Rome, which was something Henry was at first reluctant to do.

You may be surprised to learn about an unlikely third party in this mix, who was the only wife Henry shared any "Confluence" with and that was his first wife, Catherine of Aragon. She was born December 16, 1485, and Henry was born June 28, 1491, so like our previous example they shared around 6 months of "Partial Confluence" for every second "Significant Year". The most fateful of these periods of "Confluence" occurred in the year 1522, when Catherine was in her all-important age 36 "Year of Revolution", while Henry was in his age 31 "Year of Broken Pathways".

This was the period in which Catherine hired a young, 22-year-old Anne Boleyn, to serve in attendance at Court. Boleyn had returned from four years in the French Court, where she had established a reputation as a perfect courtier - graceful, stylish and skilled at singing, dancing and playing the lute.

It would have been small wonder if Boleyn hadn't caught Henry's eye, but she made her feelings known early on, that she wasn't interested in being a mistress. Henry's quest to resolve this impasse represented his challenge and uphill struggle, that consumed him for many years and became known as 'The King's Great Matter'. On the other hand, I'm sure if Catherine had been able to see what might happen, she would have ensured that this charming, but steely, young girl never got employed.

This was to usher in her new age and ultimately lead to her downfall. The marriage of Henry and Catherine has been described as "unusually good" in spite of Henry's affairs, which Catherine seemed to tolerate. Thus, both their friendship and her forbearance were on display.

Though not quite as well-known, the relationship and suspected marriage of Catherine The Great of Russia and her courtier Grigory Potemkin (which sometimes gets included on all-time couples lists), also falls into the category of not being "Confluent", but having an equal measure of love and attraction to power (particularly on his part). In modern times a good example of such a relationship would be Bill and Hillary Clinton.

I can hear many of you thinking to yourselves at this point, "yes, that's fairly interesting, but knocking the dust off all this ancient history isn't what I want to hear about. What about today's high profile relationships, both good and bad?" Well, I can assure you that I'm going to address at least a sample of these in coming chapters.

From my perspective, it is a lot easier to have completed biographies to study. After all, almost anything can and sometimes does happen in affairs of the heart. As I mentioned previously, simply being "Confluent" with another prospective person, does not mean instant compatibility or even any compatibility at all.

It must be combined with that essential spark. You may also have just that same spark with a person who shares no period of "Confluence" with you. As I told you at the outset, I do not promise a silver bullet and I may end up muddying the waters of love and romance still more.

What I want you to see though is the sheer statistical unlikelihood of the presence of "Confluence" in just about every 'All-Time Famous Couples List' I have explored. Granted there are some notable exceptions like Edward VIII and Wallis Simpson, but there are way more matches than exceptions. You can see how some of them are extremely rare, and rarer still, because the famous couple actually meet in one of these very narrow bands of months, that I call "Windows of Opportunity" and therefore classifies them as having a "Fated Relationship".

Most statistical studies of the age discrepancy of marriage partners tell you that partners born less than a year apart, constitute around a 12-13% slice of their total sample. For periods of 10+ years discrepancy (i.e., a lot of the cases I have dealt with), we are dealing with less than a 1% probability for this large block of years.

For individual years, such as 12 or 24 or 36 (along with the most detailed supporting evidence), it becomes a very small part of that 1% and for shared periods of these years, as I have illustrated, it is infinitesimally small. Yet into this table of averages, I have demonstrated somewhere between 50-75% of matches with established lists of famous couples.

This is a hugely unlikely possibility. At least, nominally, a one-in-a-thousand chance for each separate, single 10+ years case. So, the likelihood of randomly finding four consecutive data matches out of a list of 10, with a single year of a 10+ age discrepancy; such as JFK and Jackie, Bogie and Bacall, Chaplin and O'Neill, and Juan and Eva Peron would be 1 in 1,000 x 1,000 x 1,000 x 1,000, which is 1 in a trillion!

Like everything else about "Life Cycles Theory", it challenges all rational explanations and directly defies prevailing wisdom, which says there are no meaningful coincidences and all data is simply randomly distributed. This also leaves aside the huge body of work I have on the "Age 36 Phenomenon" (and sometimes the age 24 "Year of Revolution"), which I have casually illustrated to you in just about every single case. No-one else has ever made a detailed study of these special coincidences, that in itself creates a powerful theoretical model.

I'll now close with a brief example of modern "Confluence" within a currently existing relationship, that of George Clooney and Amal Alamuddin. George was born May 6, 1961, and Amal was born February 3, 1978, which means they share 9 months of "Partial Confluence" for every second "Significant Year". Their whirlwind engagement before their marriage on September 27, 2014, has been extensively covered and it drew my attention, because it all occurred during Amal's important and often life-altering, age 36 "Year of Revolution".

It was also stated that George was aged 53 at the time, so unfortunately I can't also claim that this magical time in their lives happened during a rare period of "Confluence". For those who like to follow celebrity lives I can only add, that in terms of the theory, their first 9 months of "Confluence" is not due until 2021 when George will be in his age 60 "Year of Revolution" and Amal will be in her age 43 "Year of Broken Pathways".

However, both of them shared life-altering moments in their respective age 36 "Years of Revolution". In Amal's case, she was introduced to George at a charity event in September, 2013. She was reluctant to follow up because of his reputation, but they shared a meal in the next month, although assistants denied they were dating.

The first public evidence of a relationship happened in mid-February, 2014 (in other words at the beginning of Amal's age 36 year). This was when they held hands at the White House screening of Clooney's movie. He proposed to her only 2 months later. So far, this looks like very plain sailing, however the theory would say there should be a "Moment of Frustration/Setback" before the final "Moment of Breakthrough".

This, in fact, happened in July when the *Daily Mail* published a story saying that Amal's mother opposed the marriage on religious grounds and had been spreading this around their Muslim community in Beirut. Clooney was irate and claimed that family members were "put in harm's way" and accused the newspaper of "inciting violence".

This caused the *Daily Mail* to issue a public apology for any distress caused. Amal is actually from the Druze sect, which is nominally classified as one of the five Muslim sects, but in reality is a Unitarian religion, embracing other faiths as well. In addition, Amal's mother is not even a member of the sect.

So there is no doubt, this is prima facie evidence of a "Moment of Setback/Frustration". Her wonderful wedding in September was also, no doubt, her "Moment of Breakthrough". In addition, her career highlights included being appointed to the UK Public International Law Panel for a period of five years in February, 2014, as well as being chosen as Barbara

Walter's 'Most Fascinating Person of 2014'.

If we take George's age 36 year, we are left with a very interesting question. The sort I regularly ask myself, whenever I get a brainwave. "Now you don't know much, if anything, about Clooney's career except he first found fame on the TV show *E.R.*, and then in the movies. So in the period May 1997 to May 1998 (when he was aged 36), did he have some sort of breakthrough and did he have a setback before this?" Most of my research looks so calm and rational afterward, but before I do it, I'm anything but calm.

George Clooney's life was dominated by two movies during this time. The first was *Batman & Robin,* starring Clooney as Batman and released in June, 1997. Only true fans of the Batman franchise and Clooney himself should know this, but this movie turned out to be a disaster. It was a critical failure, receiving an embarrassing 11% on the critical review site *Rotten Tomatoes* and has been called one of the worst movies of all time. It ended any chance of a sequel until 2005 and *The San Francisco Chronicle* said, "George Clooney is the big zero of the film".

Clooney can be seen still apologising for destroying Batman on a 2015 TV chat show. Suffice it to say, this constituted a Grade A "Moment of Setback/Frustration" and would have done his fledgling movie career, begun in 1996, no favours. He had to get things back on track.

During the period of 1997 and early 1998, he was filming *Out of Sight,* described as a criminal comedy. Did he do better this time? The answer is a big yes. It was a critical success scoring 93% on *Rotten Tomatoes* and receiving several Academy Award nominations.

Clooney's performance was praised with one noted critic saying, "Clooney has never been better...at last he looks like a big screen star; the good-looking leading man from television is over with." George also said it was one of his favourite films on his resume. So there you have it. A perfect illustration of both objective (i.e., press reports/articles) and subjective (i.e., the person's own words) evidence of the "Age 36 Phenomenon".

I can assure you that there is much more material like this to come. I will be unveiling a workshop example on the Brad Pitt/Angelina Jolie/Jennifer Aniston scandal from a "Life Cycles Theory" point of view. It will be an instance of my final theoretical term - a "Whorl of Confluence". I will then discuss other cases like the founders of Google - Larry Page and Sergey Brin, along with Brin's former wife, Anne Wojcicki.

So many household names will be used from a wide variety of fields. Everyone from the Wright Brothers and Abraham Lincoln to Star Trek, to the crazy love life of John Cleese; from Armstrong, Aldrin and Collins to Tom Cruise's three marriages. If you think you know a fair bit of trivia, I guarantee to expand your knowledge many times over, and if you like to delve into endless fascinating tales of the lives of others, then sit back and get comfortable. Finally, I aim to overwhelm you with the most dramatic "Life Cycles Theory" evidence ever presented.

CHAPTER FIVE

CAREERS AND CONFLUENCE

This is the first of several chapters illustrating my many case studies in this brand new aspect of "Life Cycles Theory". I admit that there may always be some overlap with the areas of family, friendship and romance, because these divisions are a little artificial, but I will try my best to keep matters separate.

The world of work and careers can often see us closely involved with others in a way that also brings us together as friends and colleagues. Sometimes it is a result of a long-term formal arrangement, like your immediate work unit, and other times it can be a one-off project that involves us intensely for a shorter time. People in these work-related situations will then be linked to the period of "Confluence" that they share.

As I did in the last chapter, I should stress that successful and enjoyable teamwork need not involve any "Confluence" at all and in some cases people who are strongly "Confluent" can turn out to be each other's worst enemies. My examples are in no way intended to be comprehensive, they are based more on the intrinsic entertainment value of the story. There are no lists to reference here, as no-one really studies the 'great career partnerships of all time'.

With that said, let's begin with the very well-known 1969 Moon Landing. The death of Neil Armstrong in 2012 brought arguably the greatest achievement of the twentieth century into public focus once again. The Moon Mission was a very high-profile example of "Confluence" in a special project team.

So, this being the case, let's do a little analysis of the Moon Mission team, shall we? Neil Armstrong was born August 5, 1930, Buzz Aldrin was born January 20, 1930, and Michael Collins was born October 31, 1930. What does this tell you? Yes, they were all "Confluent" with each other for every "Significant Year" in their combined lives. This should make an ideal combination for a small hand-picked team. The risks of not returning to earth during this voyage were large and ultimate success depended on close collaboration and improvisation.

For example, some may remember how much drama they had to face, when during the landing Neil Armstrong had to take over manual control of the Lunar Module to find a suitable place to land and they almost ran out of fuel. What you probably don't know is that when they climbed back into the module for lift off, the ignition switch for the ascent engine was broken accidentally by their bulky spacesuits and part of a pen had to be used to activate the launch sequence. A great example of life-saving improvisation, if ever there was one.

It should be stated that though the famous trio were good friends, who enjoyed catching up every five years for a presidential reunion, they were not particularly close. However, reports of a rift between Aldrin and Armstrong over who walked on the moon first were proven to be inaccurate. I am always happy to share my findings, even if I was hoping to hear of lifelong close friendships.

Now let's dig a bit further into their one relevant period of "Confluence" in their combined age 36 "Years of Revolution" (end October, 1966 to end January, 1967). Let's set up a hypothesis for testing. You can see this did not coincide with the moon landing. So what did happen that could be considered a reasonable turning point in their careers? Well, on January 27, 1967, Apollo 1, designed to be the first lunar spaceship, caught fire on the launch pad, killing astronauts Grissom, White and Chaffee.

After the inquest on April 5, a group of 17, including obviously Armstrong, Aldrin and Collins, were told, "the guys who are going to fly the first lunar missions are the guys in this room." This was to be the new age/directions for the eventual team and directly lead to the Moon Mission in 1969. For Armstrong, Aldrin and Collins it was to become one of the most memorable team achievements in modern history.

By way of contrast, we'll now travel back to arguably the best known US President, Abraham Lincoln. I'm going to provide one of the most detailed and precise calculations I've ever undertaken with "Confluence". This centres on Lincoln's early life when he was in his age 36 "Year of Revolution". Here's a question for you, "what happens if we put two serious and career-minded 36-year-old individuals of roughly the same ability, together, when they are aiming for the same job?"

Well, it happened when prairie lawyer and state politician, Abraham

Lincoln, was running against volunteer soldier and national politician, General John J. Hardin, to be nominated for a term in Congress. Now here's where it gets mathematical. Lincoln was born February 12, 1809, and Hardin was born January 5, 1810, which means they were both 36 during the narrow window of one month (between January 5 and February 12, 1846). Why this matters is because they were both aiming for the same job during this time i.e., the Whig nomination for a 2-year term in Congress.

Hardin had already served one term and it was Lincoln who introduced the principle of rotation, meaning that it would be his turn next. He had never been elected to Congress. Hardin, like many other politicians, did not abide by this gentleman's agreement and so in 1845 they fought a spirited contest. They were also friends, so things were bound to get sticky. My question is simple, "when was this nomination settled?" Was it during the one month period of "Confluence" that the two shared in January 1846? Did it seal both their careers and ultimate fates? I have the *Lincoln Log* of his voluminous correspondence for research purposes.

It says explicitly that the matter was not settled at the start of the year. Then, in January, Lincoln did some dedicated campaigning and won several key districts. Hardin could see the writing on the wall and eventually, in early February, he formally withdrew his candidacy.

Yes, this one month of January where the two shared "Confluence" is when it all happened. Both being at their major midlife "Years of Revolution" together. Both ambitious and talented members of the same Whig party and both wanting to be Congressman. This sealed both their fates at the one time.

Why so? Well, it began Lincoln's first term in Washington. His quest for influence and his growing distaste for slavery now saw the beginnings of a credible national profile. He co-wrote a bill to abolish slavery in the District of Columbia and spoke out against the Mexican War. Hardin, on the other hand, returned to the Illinois Militia and recruited the First Volunteer Regiment to fight in the Mexican-American War. On February 23, 1847, he was killed at the Battle of Buena Vista, just one year later. His untimely demise weighed on Lincoln thereafter, and as President he looked out for Hardin's widow and appointed his brother-in-law to a diplomatic post in Panama.

I have much more unpublished material on the whole of Lincoln's life, but I'll keep to my terms of reference. However, there is one more fascinating intersect in a "Significant Year" in the same shared month of January between

Lincoln and Hardin, that I think you will enjoy.

If we look at the period of "Confluence" when both men were in their age 31 "Year of Broken Pathways" (i.e., January, 1841 to February, 1841), we see a traumatic time in young Lincoln's life. He was due to marry Mary Todd on January 1, 1841, but had apparently changed his mind and failed to show up. According to the owner of Edwards Mansion, where the ceremony was to take place, "he went crazy as a loon," because of the shame he had caused his eventual wife, Mary.

In January, when Lincoln suffered a prolonged bout of melancholia, Hardin took over the leadership of the Whigs in the legislature. This gave him a platform on which to later succeed for a term in Congress. So you can see how this one month period of "Confluence" changed both their lives and careers at 31 and 36.

Of passing interest also, it was Hardin who intervened in a duel between Lincoln and James Shields in 1842. He arrived just before it was due to start and simply said, "this is all nonsense," after which both parties backed down.

"FULL CONFLUENCE" PERIOD: JAN. TO FEB. OF FOLLOWING YEAR (1 MONTH)

LINCOLN

DOB: 12.02.1809

HARDIN

DOB: 9.01.1810

	LINCOLN'S AGE	EVENT	HARDIN'S AGE	
	31	When Lincoln doesn't attend his wedding he suffers a bout of melancholia. Hardin takes over leadership of the Whig Party.	31	
	36	Lincoln wins key support in election for his first term in Washington and Hardin withdraws. Defines the fate of both men.	36	

Changing gears to a less weighty topic I'll now explore the amazing amount of "Confluence" between cast members of the hit TV Series, *The Seinfeld Show*. In 2002, Time magazine nominated *The Seinfeld Show*, as the greatest sitcom in the history of TV. Now that's debatable, but what's not debatable is that it was a worldwide phenomenon that makes people of just about every country and culture laugh. I think there'll always be reruns on cable.

Jerry was born April 29, 1954. I have previously demonstrated that *The Seinfeld Show* properly began during his age 36 "Year of Revolution", which is yet another valid and well-known case. It also ended when he was in his age 43 "Year of Broken Pathways", so the whole unbroken path of seven years is on display. This time, however, we're going to be looking at other cast members to see what their "Confluence" was like to Jerry and to each other.

Firstly, Jason Alexander (George Costanza) was born September 23, 1959, which means that he is "Confluent" with Jerry for seven months in every second shared "Significant Year". The last pairing of Jason at 31 and Jerry at 36, was right in the period when *The Seinfeld Show* was properly launched as a midseason replacement in early 1991. So *The Seinfeld Show* was born in "Confluence". Jerry and George are shown as the two closest buddies in the show and are also the best of friends in real life, so this is a good example of "Confluence" in both work and friendship.

Now let's examine Julia Louis-Dreyfus (Elaine Benes). She was born January 13, 1961. This means she shared 3½ months of "Confluence" with Jerry in every second "Significant Year". So Julia was in her important age 36 "Year of Revolution" at the same time as Jerry was in his age 43 "Year of Broken Pathways". This coincided exactly with the finish of the show. Julia and Jerry were also work mates and good buddies, and the finish of the show happened at a fateful time in both their lives.

Finally, let's visit the most out-there member of our famous quartet, actor and comedian Michael Richards (Cosmo Kramer), who was born July 24, 1949. This makes him also "Confluent" with Jerry for nine months of every second "Significant Year". In their case when the show closed, it was in Richards' age 48 "Year of Revolution", as well as Jerry's age 43 "Year of Broken Pathways". In addition, Richards and Louis-Dreyfus were "Confluent" for around six months of every "Significant Year". So according to the theory of "Confluence", they should have a natural empathy with both each other and with Jerry.

I realise this type of analysis, with several people involved, becomes quite detailed once you get going, but the bottom line is they all shared a strong degree of "Confluence", which must have made working together a dream. *The Seinfeld Show* was properly launched in "Confluence" and it most certainly ended in a period of "Confluence" with three out of the four of them in a "Significant Year" at the time.

Turning now to world famous scientific teams, I will explore the "Confluence" present in the duo who cracked the DNA code, namely James Watson and Francis Crick. It often seems that working teams will be around the same age range, so it was an interesting discovery for me to find that these two household-name scientists were, in fact, separated by a 12-year age gap. You should, of course, know by now that this would make them "Confluent".

Francis Crick was the elder of the two being born June 8, 1916 and James Watson was born April 26, 1928. This makes them "Confluent" for 10½ months out of a possible 12. In other words, there was a near-universal coverage. The next question then becomes, "did any of this relate to their pioneering research?" The period we will be looking at was when Crick was in his major midlife, age 36 "Year of Revolution" and Watson was in his first adult, age 24 "Year of Revolution" (i.e., early June, 1952 to late April, 1953).

Just prior to this period Crick had been working on X-Ray diffraction of a helical molecule. In late 1951, he was joined at the University of Cambridge by a young 23-year-old American, James Watson, who already had a Ph.D. They shared an interest in learning how genetic information might be stored in molecular form. A key piece of data was X-ray diffraction images, but their first attempt to find a molecular model of DNA had not been successful.

Also working in this area was famous US scientist Linus Pauling and he had planned to visit the UK in May, 1952 (in other words just before the key period of "Confluence"), but because of his political activities, his travel was restricted until some months later. By the time he arrived he did not meet any notable researchers in the field and so his part in the race for DNA was looked over.

Because of their earlier failure to find the helical DNA structure, both Watson and Crick were told to do other projects and were forbidden to work in the area. This is clear evidence of a combined "Moment of Setback/Frustration".

As often happens in other areas of intense scientific interest (like splitting the atom or working on the theory of relativity) there were quite a few other players in the contest. The key theoretical breakthrough and game changer for Watson and Crick was a research chemist by the name of Rosalind Franklin. She had relevant data, but when she left for a new position, she had threatened to give it to (you guessed it) Linus Pauling.

This suddenly sparked permission for a new second attempt by Watson and Crick, who were given her data to work with, without her permission. This was also undoubtedly their combined "Moment of Breakthrough", because they went on to discover their double helix model in February 1953 and publish it soon after. The press simplified it with an article, "Why you are you. The secret of life." It was called the DNA scientific revolution and yes, it all happened squarely in the critical "Window of Opportunity" for 36-year-old Francis Crick and 24-year-old James Watson.

We're now going forward to visit the latest form of revolution in society and that is the digital information revolution. The birth of the internet was when the first web page was launched by Sir Tim Berners-Lee in August, 1991 at the CERN laboratories. In case you are a bit curious, the answer once again (with almost monotonous regularity) is yes, Tim was in his age 36 "Year of Revolution" at this time. Yes, he also had a "Moment of Setback/Frustration" when he was greeted with some initial lack-lustre press reports, but there is no doubt the information superhighway was launched.

We're going to examine some elements of the history of the dominant player in the search engine business, which is Google. So ubiquitous are they, that we usually just say 'to google' as a verb. Like most success stories though, the early days are quite interesting.

It was started by two students, Larry Page and Sergey Brin. Page was born March 26, 1973 and Brin's date of birth was August 21, 1973, which by now you can easily discern, showed they shared a fair amount of "Confluence" (it was a full 7 months between late August and late March of the following year).

Did you know that the Google concept was born in a dream by Larry Page? If not, you should just google it and hear Larry's story in his own words. Now I've got to admit that this significant moment was not in one of his "Significant Years" (he was aged 22 at the time), so the question I am faced with is, "what does Larry and Sergey's combined period of "Confluence" (when both were in their age 24 "Years of Revolution") have to do with their fledgling careers with Google?"

This is the period late August, 1997 to late March, 1998. By now Larry and Sergey, who actually didn't get well at first, had decided to combine their complementary strengths with a single aim - to sell this very exciting search engine concept for a million dollars to whoever was willing to buy it. At the end of 1997, (in other words right in the middle of this key period) they offered it to Yahoo, who decided to pass. These days Google is valued at around 10 times what Yahoo is worth.

This period also contained the birth of the Google name by accident. Larry had initially picked Googol (because it represents 1 followed by 100 zeros, to reflect the immense volume of data they wished to store), but their first donor cheque of $100,000 misspelled it Google and they had to create a bank account with that name, so they could cash it.

Interestingly, once Larry and Sergey began to work together, they grew to become very close and went on to be lifelong best friends, showing the strong empathy implied in their large amount of "Confluence".

Let's travel along our universal path of 7 years of "Unbroken Forward Momentum" from their combined age 24 "Years of Revolution" to their combined age 31 "Years of Broken Pathway" (i.e., late August, 2004 to late March, 2005). This is really straightforward, because it was when Google went public in August, 2004, making the two founders instant paper billionaires.

By comparison it was at the same age (and following a 7 year company journey) that Bill Gates did the same with Microsoft. Yes, I've studied many leading figures in the IT industry, as you're finding out.

Their final period of "Confluence", at the time of writing, was their combined age 36 important midlife "Years of Revolution" (i.e., late August, 2009 to late March, 2010). This period represented an important new stage in each of their lives (as the theory would predict), but it was quite different in nature for each. It would help to define their own individual career reputations.

Let's go firstly to Larry. He has been compared to Steve Jobs, who was famously forced out of Apple by investors dissatisfied with his abrasive management style. Now Larry, who was the prime mover in Google, also had a somewhat difficult, introverted nature and in 2001 investors insisted an outsider be brought in as CEO.

That person was Eric Schmidt, and because he was 20 years older than Larry and Sergey, the term 'adult supervision' was used. Larry didn't leave, but he became more remote in day-to-day terms. However, he was still front and centre with product development.

As time went by, he began to want to come in from the management cold more strongly, to reclaim his birthright as it were. The reality was that he had always been a control freak and he still believed he, together with Sergey, were the only ones to run Google. This goal was about to be realised with the Android project. It began with the success of the iPhone launch in 2007. The next year, in September 2008, a Larry Page-led project team introduced an iPhone knock-off product, to be known as Android. It was free for phone makers to install.

In mid-2009 (i.e., at the early part of Larry's age 36 year) Android had captured only 1.8% market share; however during the exact period in question (i.e., second half 2009 to early 2010), Android went on to get 17.2% of the market, toppling iPhone at 14%. Page had, as a manager, produced and delivered the world's most popular mobile phone operating system. He had truly come of age. Other factors, combined with Page's new maturity and success as a manager, resulted in Schmidt resigning as CEO in January, 2011. This was to be what his personal and career-defining central age 36 "Year of Revolution" was all about.

In order to analyse Sergey's age 36 "Year of Revolution", I've got to introduce one more significant person, who shared an almost equal amount of "Confluence" with both Larry and Sergey. This is Sergey's former wife, Anne Wojcicki. Anne Wojcicki was born July 28, 1973, so she shares an amazing 11 out of a possible 12 months of "Confluence". It would seem their chemistry was obvious from the very beginning in both work and romance.

In fact, they were nicknamed 'the twins' because they looked so alike and had so much in common. This is a perfect description of a strongly "Confluent" romance. It must be like meeting yourself in the form of the opposite sex. Anne has stated that she, "married her best friend".

So what happened in their first combined age 31 "Years of Broken Pathway" (August, 2004 to July, 2005)? Well, as you know, Sergey became very wealthy overnight, but this also coincided with his mother's diagnosis of Parkinson's disease. As a biotech analyst, Anne now had a personal as well as professional interest in the whole matter. This was to mark the beginning of the Brin Wojcicki Foundation, with an initial $100,000 donation to the Michael J Fox Foundation. They are committed to finding a cure for Parkinson's disease.

Meanwhile, the Brin Wojcicki Foundation still exists, separate to their new status as divorcees and has very substantial assets, with around $1 billion + in funds. It has become a centrepiece of their shared goals to fund Parkinson's research ($160 million over the last 4 years) and a variety of other social change initiatives. So their shared quest begins when both are in their age 31 "Years of Broken Pathways".

Now we are finally going to look at their combined age 36 "Years of Revolution" (August, 2009 to July, 2010). Firstly to Sergey. His interests and vision has always been wider than Google (like space travel and robots who can become our friends - the 'cool stuff' as he calls it), but ever since he received his diagnosis of a strong chance of acquiring Parkinson's disease at some stage (potentially even within 10 years), it has become a major focus of his life. He exercises religiously, drinks coffee which he doesn't enjoy, etc. Basically, any measures that can decrease his risk factor.

In mid-2009 (the start of Sergey's and Anne's "Confluent" period), thanks to support from Google and their Foundation, Anne's company 23andMe assembled its Parkinson's disease research initiative by analysing data from 3,400 patients. They replicated some known genetic associations, but also identified two new novel loci, with the results published in PLOS Genetics in 2011. They worked with the Cleveland Clinic to get their volunteer subjects and when joined to a wider sample of 6,500, it became the largest cohort of Parkinson's patients in the world to be tested.

So it becomes obvious when you put the pieces together. Sergey and Anne actually shared the positive basis of their combined age 36 "Years of Revolution". This is simply to one day find a cure for this crippling genetic disease - Parkinson's. It was done through Anne's company and Sergey's backing by Google and their Foundation.

It will directly benefit him, of course, but as he points out, it will benefit many, many others. After all, if you are a real futurist like Sergey, you'd want to live a long time to see some of your wackier plans take shape.

Given that Anne has been fighting for the survival of 23andMe ever since the FDA started investigating in 2009, this research with the Cleveland Clinic started at the same time could, one day, become the weapon that the company needs to secure legitimacy in the US.

This brings me now to their own personal life. What happens when you divorce your twin, as it were? Well, it often means that the friendship side of "Confluence" still persists and all your shared experiences still bind you together. Currently, Sergey and Anne still live close by, so he can have easy access to their children and they continue their work with their Foundation and its support of 23andMe.

Both Sergey and Anne may have dated others, but I've got news for them. "Confluence" would say they'll never meet anyone more empathic and understanding than each other, committed to mutually supportive goals. The veritable definition of what closeness and lifelong friendship is all about. Small wonder that Larry (who remember is "Confluent" with both of them) was furious when he heard the news of Sergey's office romance with Amanda Rosenberg, which led to his divorce.

As one Google insider stated, "Larry is so ethically strict. I heard he was insanely upset by this whole situation and wasn't talking to Sergey." Of course, he would be. Two of his closest friends. This whole analysis has been a very valuable study of just how people behave, who share so much "Confluence".

My last example is a very interesting and rare case of predictions and "Life Cycles Theory". As you know I subscribe to free will and as such, we are always capable of changing our minds and doing the unexpected. I, along with everyone else, obviously don't know exactly what will happen; but where I have studied a famous life in detail, I can make an educated guess about when something might happen.

This occurred with the well-known author J.K. Rowling, whose life I studied and wrote about in considerable detail. Indeed, she was one of my major teaching examples in Book Two. I had proceeded as far as I could then, which was up to her age 43 "Year of Broken Pathways" and even a couple of years beyond. I was aware of her approaching age 48 "Year of Revolution", when several years ago, I heard a chance piece of news about a brand new project for Rowling. You may be wondering what all this has to do with "Confluence", so I'll keep you in suspense no longer.

This was about a brand new film franchise deal, which was announced in the second half of 2013. It set up an exact hypothesis for testing in Rowling's life, at the time I researched it. You see she just turned 48 in July, 2013. The news report talked of a brand new Harry Potter spin-off franchise deal, being signed with Warner Bros.

Why was this a new direction? Well, Rowling was to become a screenwriter for the first time. Also, there would be no Harry Potter and no Daniel Radcliffe. It was going to centre around a character called Newt Scamander, who comes from a Potter textbook by the name of *Fantastic Beasts*

And Where To Find Them. This book is only 41 pages long and was first published in November, 2001, when Rowling was in her age 36 "Year of Revolution".

Although the main game for her at 36 was the release of the first Harry Potter movie, marking the beginning of her then new age/direction, it was also to serve as an unlikely 12-year journey from *Fantastic Beasts* being published as a textbook, to its new conception as a screenplay during her age 48 "Year of Revolution".

This deal was not initiated by Rowling either and this is where the unlikely period of "Confluence" comes in. It was the brainchild of the new CEO at Warner's, one Kevin Tsujihara. He was also 48 when he became CEO (October, 2012 to October, 2013) and he saw the potential in this project. Others at Warner's didn't think he could woo talent, because of his low-profile background in the distribution side of the business and Rowling was notoriously difficult to negotiate with. It took many months of courting her attorney and agent in the UK and she had to be sweet-talked into the deal.

She was demanding creative control and would have to approve any rewrites. It was the one successful screenwriting team, who had done all the Potter movies, and Rowling had never done any screenwriting before. The studio bosses were understandably a bit nervous.

The question then becomes, "what was the combined period of "Confluence" for Tsujihara and Rowling?" It was from July 31, 2013 to October 25, 2013, a period of only three months and the deal was announced in the last week of September, 2013, which was right in the middle of this very narrow "Window of Opportunity" for these two very disparate lives. This is an excellent example of careers suddenly overlapping in a pivotal way during a period of "Confluence".

It was stated the original deal was for a franchise of three *Fantastic Beasts* movies, provided of course that they were commercially successful, but this has since been extended to five. There has also been a fair number of media releases and hype surrounding the first movie, due to come out literally as I am writing this passage, so it would seem its initial success is almost guaranteed. This will, no doubt, see the ushering in of a very significant new era in the careers of both J.K. Rowling and Kevin Tsujihara.

After taking a short break, I can now say that the release of *Fantastic Beasts* has just happened, with both critics and the public alike calling it, "a hit". Leading review site *Rotten Tomatoes* gave it a 75% average, with comments such as, "draws on Harry Potter's rich mythology to deliver a spinoff that dazzles with franchise-building magic of its own." So far, it has grossed around $500 million on a budget of $180 million, so this franchise could be described as off and running.

I hope all these disparate examples, of small intersecting corners of some very well-known lives, has given you food for thought about the possibility of "Confluence" operating and influencing important career turning points in your own life. It certainly did for me when I examined the long relationship I had with my first boss. It turned out we were almost totally "Confluent" at a 12-year interval (about 11½ out of a possible 12 months).

This, at first, produced considerable empathy and friendship, but when another colleague joined, who was also equally "Confluent" with both of us, it all turned sour and became a clash of personalities. This colleague and I have been lifelong friends, so I guess something had to give.

You can readily see how boundaries between chapters will overlap as careers often involve important friendships, as well as family members, on occasion. However, we'll continue to proceed on the basis of the intrinsic interest value of the stories. By the way all you trivia buffs, how are you doing with all this detail? You are, of course, forgiven for not knowing it and my promise to vastly increase selective areas of your general knowledge will continue to hold good.

CHAPTER SIX

FAMILY, FRIENDS AND CONFLUENCE

There is no more formative influence in our early lives than our immediate families. The question I wish to raise is, what happens when in addition to all the benefits of a supportive family environment (for those fortunate enough to enjoy one), we also have the presence of "Confluence"? The extra bond of empathy and understanding is implied, along with the special "Windows of Opportunity" that can arise during the overlap of "Significant Years".

The first case I want to discuss is one of the best-known pairs of brothers in world history, Wilbur and Orville Wright. I came upon this amazing discovery by chance one day, when I was visiting the National Air and Space Museum in Washington, DC. I overheard a person in front of me in the queue being told to visit the Historical Exhibit first because it was about to close.

I duly took this advice and ran into various items to do with the Wright Brothers history making, heavier-than-air flight on December 17, 1903. I then saw that Wilbur, the elder of the two brothers, was born April 16, 1867. I quickly added 36 onto the 1867 year and there it was again, another high-profile correlation of outstanding achievement, happening in a person's age 36 "Year of Revolution". One more milestone for me and a stark reminder of the sheer depth of my research data on this one single correlation.

But this chapter is to do with "Confluence" in families and not merely another opportunity to skite about the "Age 36 Phenomenon". It was then that I chanced upon the younger of the two brothers, Orville, to discover that he was born August 19, 1871. This means they shared four months of "Confluence" in every second "Significant Year".

More importantly, it means that just before the flight was made, Orville was in his age 31 "Year of Broken Pathways", while Wilbur was in his age 36 "Year of Revolution". This made me want to drill down into the exact period in which they shared "Confluence" (i.e., April to August, 1903). This was their "Window of Opportunity" period.

In summary, during 1903, the brothers built the powered Wright Flyer I, using their preferred material for construction, spruce, a strong and lightweight wood. I will now create a timeline for these events. On February, 12-13, they tested an unsuccessful engine whose body and frame cracked during testing. Then Wilbur made a March, 1903 entry in his notebook indicating the prototype propeller was only 66% efficient. So just prior to our period of "Confluence" (April-August) things were not complete. We all know a powered airplane needs a workable engine and though they almost had their design done, it wouldn't succeed without it.

The Wrights next wrote to several engine manufacturers, but none met their need for a sufficiently lightweight power plant. They then turned to their shop mechanic, Charlie Taylor, who built an engine in just six weeks in close consultation with the brothers. To keep the weight low enough, the engine block was cast from aluminum, a rare practice for the time.

The Wright-Taylor engine had no fuel pump, carburettor, or spark plugs. Nor did it have a throttle. Yet this simple motor produced 12 horsepower, an acceptable margin above the Wrights' minimum requirement of 8 horsepower. It was patented on May 22, 1903. So now in this "Window of Opportunity" period preparations were properly underway.

Things were largely completed by August (i.e., by the end of the period of "Confluence"), because in September they arrived in Kill Devil Hills and in October they commenced assembling it. It should be noted that their airplane - The Flyer - cost less than a thousand dollars, in contrast to more than $50,000 in government funds, that was given to their rival Samuel Langley, for his man-carrying Great Aerodrome project.

He was trying to beat them to the punch at precisely the same time. You know what? Langley gave up the project after two crashes at takeoff on October 7 and December 8, 1903. There's destiny if ever there was. If I'd been around then, I'd have said, "put your money on the 36-year-old Wilbur Wright, not the 69-year-old Samuel Langley". He's not in any sort of "Significant Year". This also says something about the sheer tenacity and eventual superiority of the solo underfunded pioneers.

Leaving aside siblings, I will now turn my attention to one of my most often studied family relationships and that is parent and child. I have found my frame of reference here has usually been where there is a common "Year of Revolution" involved. One that I am particularly interested in is the bond between a parent in their age 36 "Year of Revolution" and their child. Since the age of 36 is so pivotal in many lives, it is interesting to see how things unfold.

One case I've studied in detail has been the famous Tiffany family. There are two very well-known branches of this family. The first is the jewellery shops headquartered in New York. As of 2014, it was operating 121 stores in the Americas, 72 in Asia-Pacific, 54 in Japan, 37 in Europe, and 5 in emerging markets. It seems so well-established today that you will probably be amazed at how father Charles got it all started. The second branch belongs to the iconic Tiffany glassware, founded by equally famous son, Louis.

Charles Lewis Tiffany was born February 15, 1812, and he began a stationery and gift shop in New York with his partner, John B. Young, when he was just past his age 24 "Year of Revolution" by a couple of months. Their takings for the first three days were only $4.38. Things improved as they started to add a range of giftware products over the next several years. However, my central question always was, "what happened to represent a life-changing new direction in his age 36 "Year of Revolution" (i.e., most of the year 1848)?"

OK then, here we go. In the year 1848 there was much turmoil in France generally, and the city of Paris in particular. It was known as the February Revolution, resulting in the end of the Orleans monarchy and by year's end, the establishment of the French Second Republic. But to Charles Tiffany, who had recently sent a representative to Paris to buy and import a range of fine giftware, this spelled opportunity. I am quoting from the *Biographical Dictionary of America, Vol. 10,*

> *"In 1848 the firm began the manufacture of gold jewelry. During the panic that followed the disturbances in France in 1848, diamonds declined fifty percent, and Mr. Tiffany invested all the available resources of the firm in the purchase of these gems. They consequently became the largest diamond merchants in the country."*

So here we have more landmark evidence. The very thing that Charles Tiffany became known for happened in 1848, not in 1837 when he opened a stationery and gift store. It was, no doubt, preceded by a "Moment of Frustration" as he had to deal with the day-to-day vagaries of life in the war-torn French capital, as well as putting all his money on the line. But this is again more trumpet-blowing from my side. Just what does it have to do with "Confluence" in families?

The answer is everything really, for his even more famous son, Louis Comfort Tiffany, was born February 18, 1848. Thus father and son shared almost 100% "Confluence" with the added advantage of it happening during a parent's all-important, life-changing and reputation-making, age 36 "Year of Revolution". This should make them amazingly empathic and supportive of each other's needs. Let's now visit the same two central "Years of Revolution" (i.e., at 24 and 36) in Louis' life.

He was in his age 24 "Year of Revolution" for most of 1872. He exhibited his first watercolour painting during this time, but more importantly, he began to work with glass in this year. This is significant because it is what he would become famous for. I'm now going to quote from a book called *Art Nouveau* by Jean Lahor,

> *"Tiffany first became interested in working with glass in 1872, at the age of 24, with the funding and support of his father's business. Although Louis quickly became an expert in the glassmaking field, he continued to sell his picturesque oil and watercolor paintings for the next seven years At the age of thirty-one he started an interior decorating firm with a number of other specialists."* (NB, here again we see the seven years of "Unbroken Forward Momentum" to his age 31 "Year of Broken Pathways")

Most importantly though, we also see direct evidence of his father's active support of his son, not in learning the jewellery business (as he was hoping for), but in his son's chosen field of art and glassmaking. His father (who was aged 60 by then) never pressed him to take over the business but lent his support both financially and in other ways. For example, when Louis opened his interior decorating business, it was with some of his father's influential clients. This led onto a high point of the small firm receiving a commission to redecorate a section of the White House.

When Louis was in his pivotal age 36 "Year of Revolution" (most of the year 1884), he dissolved his interior decorating business, Associated Artists, and took steps to form his own glass factory in Corona, New York, determined to provide the designs that improved the quality of contemporary glass. His leadership and talent together with his father's backing saw the business, known as the Tiffany Glass Company (opened in 1885), thrive and secure a very prominent and unique place in the Art Nouveau world.

Here it is again. The genesis of the thing that Louis became known for happened in his age 36 "Year of Revolution" and again it involved the financial backing of his father, Charles. It should be pointed out that Louis' wife, Mary Goddard (whom he married at 24) died in 1884, leaving him very distressed for some time. Here is another well-documented "Moment of Setback/Frustration" (along with arguments with his then business partners), preceding the "Moment of Achievement/Breakthrough" that I constantly write about.

It should also be noted that it was his father, Charles (his best friend and confidant), who was most concerned about his welfare at this time and sought to have him design and live in a section of his own new sprawling residence, the Tiffany Mansion, at 72nd and Madison. This is displayed for you below.

"FULL CONFLUENCE" PERIOD: FEB. TO FEB. OF FOLLOWING YEAR (12 MONTHS)

CHARLES TIFFANY	CHARLES TIFFANY'S AGE	EVENT	LOUIS TIFFANY'S AGE	LOUIS TIFFANY
DOB: 15.02.1812	60	Louis begins working with glass and displays watercolour painting. Charles supports him even though he would prefer him to take over the family business.	24	DOB: 18.02.1848
	67	Louis begins interior decorating business with some of his father's clients.	31	
	72	Louis dissolves the interior decorating firm and sets up the Tiffany Glass Company again with his father's financial backing. He also gets Louis to design and live in part of his large home after his wife dies.	36	

This is a wonderful story of the strong bond of "Confluence" between father and son being fully on display. I have also analysed a similar bond of "Confluence" between a father and son, who had so much shared history in the sport of boxing - Floyd Mayweather Senior and Junior. There is a recent photo of them tagged as 'Big Floyd' and 'Little Floyd', so I'll introduce them to you this way.

'Big Floyd' was born October 19, 1952, and when he was in his age 24 "Year of Revolution" (October, 1976 to October, 1977), he had a career high point of winning the U.S. Championship and also around the same time his son 'Little Floyd' was born on February 24, 1977. This means they shared eight months of "Confluence" in every "Significant Year".

There is a telling anecdote about when 'Little Floyd' was just 7-8 months old and he would mimic his father's hands in a boxing-like gesture. This caused 'Big Floyd' to say, "I knew then that he'd be a boxer!" 'Big Floyd' was a hustler and small time drug dealer at this time and his son lived with his mother and was called Floyd Sinclair.

We'll now jump to their first shared "Year of Revolution" when 'Big Floyd' was in his important age 36 year (February, 1989 to October, 1989). This was when 'Little Floyd' changed his name to Mayweather, to proudly reflect his heritage, in spite of how his father behaved, or the many beatings he gave to him. For 'Big Floyd' this period spelled just about his last fight and now a total concentration on being his son's trainer. This is, in fact, what he is best known for, so the correlation holds true once more.

When they were in their next shared "Year of Revolution", 'Big Floyd' was in his age 48 year and 'Little Floyd' was in his age 24 year (February, 2001 to October, 2001), things went decidedly pear-shaped in their relationship. Now I know it would have been perfect if they were always bonded like the Tiffanys, but I must deal with all life events, both good and bad. As I have mentioned before, people who are strongly "Confluent" can also get under each other's skin from time to time.

Well, for father and son, it was a bit worse than a bad argument. They had a falling out and 'Little Floyd' fired him as his trainer. He also evicted his father from a home that he owned and repossessed a car he was driving. They reportedly didn't have a cordial conversation for nearly seven years. This is a rather negative example of seven years of "Unbroken Forward Momentum", but it did happen.

So when 'Big Floyd' was in his age 48 "Year of Revolution" he had to watch on as his younger brother Roger (also a former World Champion boxer), took over as his son's trainer, while 'Little Floyd's' career went from strength to strength. He, in turn, began training one of his son's greatest opponents - Oscar De La Hoya.

Finally, in their last period of "Confluence" (February, 2013 to October, 2013), there is a rather magical ending to this father-son story. It is a matter of public record that in May, 2013, 'Big Floyd' again took over as his son's trainer after a break of twelve years under the steady hand of Uncle Roger. It didn't come out of thin air either. There were two factors in recent times. One was that Roger was suffering from diabetes and it affected his levels of energy.

More telling was because 'Little Floyd' felt he got hit with too many shots against Miguel Cotto, in his May 2012 fight and wanted his father's help in slipping punches. So, you can see that this duo were great examples of a "Fated Relationship", even though it was related to family and not just romance this time.

Turning now to the area of "Confluence" in friendship, a good example is the lifelong relationship, forged from the linked careers of well-known *Star Trek* actors, William Shatner and Leonard Nimoy. They first came together with the making of the original TV series, which began the whole concept.

It was started in September, 1966, but seemed doomed to an early ratings death. Critics considered it too difficult to follow and NBC would have cancelled it, except they had just begun using demographic profiling, which revealed it had a small but quality audience. They decided to give it one last shot.

Now you are forgiven for thinking, "what's any of this got to do with this chapter?" I'm sure you'll understand, however, when the details emerge. The lead actors, Leonard Nimoy and William Shatner (Captain Kirk and Mister Spock) were amazingly "Confluent" being born just 4 days apart. William was born March 22, 1931 and Leonard was born March 26, 1931, meaning they were very similar in nature to Charles and Louis Tiffany. Thus they were joined in this failing TV show and they were just about to jointly enter their important and often reputation-making age 36 "Year of Revolution" together.

NBC had ordered ten more episodes in March, 1967 (i.e., as they both were about to turn 36). When it began screening in September there was more bad news, because it was moved from its Tuesday 7:30 pm slot to Friday at 8:30 pm, when many of its young audience couldn't watch it. It came a distant second to *Gomer Pyle* and the *Friday Night Movie*. Rumours began to circulate that it was being dumped and in January, 1968, a headline exclaimed, "Star Trek Doomed. Renewal Is Unlikely".

This is the classic low point and combined "Moment of Setback/ Frustration" for both Leonard and William. Shatner was convinced the show had no future and had begun casting around for movie roles. Oddly enough, even Nimoy had been having a mildly successful musical career, singing science fiction themed songs. Remember, this would have meant no franchise, no Trekkies, no spin-offs, no movies, no Captain Kirk/Mr. Spock (except in the dustbin of entertainment trivia). So what saved *Star Trek*?

The answer was that the show's creator, Gene Roddenberry, funded the science fiction community to get a 4,000 strong letter-writing drive going. Each recipient was asked to write to NBC to save the show and send the request along to ten others.

The network received some 114,667 letters between December and March (apparently they kept count), including 52,151 in February alone. This included two Governors and several mayors and corporation heads, all pleading for the show's return. At its height the mail trucks were lined up all the way down the street. This would make a great Hollywood-style movie finish, don't you think?

It would also vindicate "Life Cycles Theory" and represent yet another combined age 36 "Moment of Breakthrough/Achievement". If I was ever challenged to display evidence, like that shown in this chapter alone, I can assure you my examples would also line up by the hundreds, and good luck to anyone who would prefer to call it just a series of fortunate coincidences and nothing more.

More important than this mutual "Moment of Breakthrough" however, William and Leonard went on to become lifelong best friends. No wonder when Leonard left us recently William said, "it was like losing my brother...he was also an amazing uncle to my daughters, etc." It's another wonderful illustration of all the positive qualities embodied in the concept of "Confluence".

For those with a good memory, I promised in Chapter Four to provide one final example from the life of Spencer Tracy, that so poignantly illustrates how an age 36 "Year of Revolution" can come to define both a life and a family. There was no question that Tracy's wife, the actress Louise Treadwell, was aware of many of his infidelities, but these were overshadowed when their son John was born profoundly deaf and doctors said it was likely he would never speak. To the very traditional Spencer, it was seen as a divine judgement on his behaviour and Louise also began to block him out and devote herself solely to her son's welfare, resulting in further strains on their marriage.

Louise was born July 31, 1897, so she was aged 36 in the period July, 1933 to July, 1934. During this time they announced to the press that they were officially separating for the only time in their long marriage. They said they would remain friends. In September, 1933, Tracy began openly dating the 20-year-old ravishing actress and his co-star, Loretta Young. She was born

January 6, 1913, and thus shared four months of "Full Confluence" with Spencer.

They were deeply in love, but shared mutual moral concerns about Spencer's marital status. She was also a strict Catholic and as Tracy would not get a divorce, she refused to begin a full relationship. Combined with her mother telling her of his alcoholism, things ended in January, 1934. He next reconciled with Louise, which came to define the rest of her life, even though Tracy's infidelities continued.

Then, in 1942, Tracy and Hepburn met and their first "Window of Opportunity" period came in the following year, when Hepburn was in her pivotal age 36 "Year of Revolution" and Tracy was in his age 43 "Year of Revolution". During this time, Louise opened a school for the deaf to help their son, John.

The John Tracy Clinic was incorporated with Walt Disney and Spencer on the original board of directors. In his opening address he said, "you honor me because I'm a movie actor, but there's nothing I have ever done that can match what Louise has done for deaf children and their parents." This caused Louise to respond with, "I will be Mrs. Spencer Tracy till the day I die," which forever defined the shape of Hepburn's 26-year-long relationship as an "open secret" in Hollywood. It is also a good illustration of how things can go one way or another in these "Window of Opportunity" periods.

It has been hypothesised that the clinic also gave Spencer a chance to redeem himself and assuage his overburdening guilt at how he continued to live. Finally, there's the most poignant postscript of all. The next day after Spencer's funeral, Katharine decided to phone Louise and suggest they could be friends. She said, "you knew him at the beginning and I at the end. I might be able to help with the kids" (who were actually aged 43 and 42 then).

Louise replied, "well yes, but I thought you were only a rumour...." That stung Katharine who later raged, "after 30 years I was only a rumour!" It was, she later wrote, "a deep and fundamental wound that never healed and by never admitting I existed, she remained the wife."

Just as I had covered a few of my many cases relating to family and friends, another high-profile instance seemed to literally overshadow current affairs media. This was the tragic deaths of *Star Wars* actress Carrie Fisher followed one day later by her mother and best friend, Debbie Reynolds. You see, I continually let current news determine which biographies I will study next, which is about as random as it gets.

I was immediately drawn to their ages at death, Carrie Fisher being 60 and Debbie Reynolds being 84. It was not the obvious and somewhat macabre correlation of both being in a "Year of Revolution", but rather it is the fact that they were almost certainly "Confluent" throughout their shared lives. It transpired that Debbie Reynolds was born April 1, 1932, and Carrie Fisher was born October 21, 1956, so they shared around 5½ months of "Confluence" for every shared "Significant Year".

So in her age 24 "Year of Revolution" she gives birth to Carrie. Next we'll look at her age 36 "Year of Revolution" (April, 1968 to April, 1969). This is often the most pivotal year in many lives, except for those who achieve their fame and reputation early, such as Reynolds. So, we are once again looking for direction-change and the birth of some new era for Reynolds in 1968/9.

Reynolds' big movie roles were all behind her by this time and she was attempting to build on her considerable TV experience with her own series, *The Debbie Reynolds Show*. It was written by the same screenwriter who created *I Love Lucy* and she was repackaged as a new look-alike version. At this stage, she also had 50% ownership and so this personal investment would have run parallel with the period when her second husband, Harry Karl, was gambling away all their combined fortunes. Much was at stake.

The show, which premiered in 1969, lasted only one season due to poor ratings and NBC's selling advertising space to tobacco companies. Reynold's hatred of smoking began after she was compelled to do it for some movie roles and was livid when she discovered what had been done on the first program. She walked away from her two-year contract and presumably most of her investment. It cost her $2 million in lost income.

She now turned to stage musicals, TV specials, and nightclub work. This was to be her new era, even if introduced in a rather negative fashion. It was unfortunately repeated some 24 years later when she was in her age 60 "Year of Revolution". At that time she purchased the Clarion Hotel and Casino in Las Vegas and renamed it the Debbie Reynolds Hollywood Hotel. It was not a success and in 1997 she was forced to declare bankruptcy.

Turning now to her daughter, Carrie Fisher, it is of interest that she found fame in her age 19 "Year of Broken Pathways", when she was cast in the original *Star Wars* movie. This was further eclipsed in her age 24 "Year of Revolution", when the hugely successful follow-up movie, *The Empire Strikes*

Back, went on to make $210 million in its initial run, from a very modest budget of $33 million. It also earned a swathe of awards at the Oscars, Golden Globes, etc. No doubt she was at the top of her game then.

Her personal life was another matter, as it has been well reported that she suffered from manic-depression (bipolar disorder) and became addicted to drugs and alcohol to help deal with this. She also had a major falling out with her mother in this era and the former very close parental bonds were well and truly broken. Now the principle of "Confluence", producing mostly great empathy and understanding, and occasionally great animosity, took hold here. The question would have been will they reconcile in the future?

At her next "Significant Year", which was her age 31 "Year of Broken Pathways", a popular book written by her called *Postcards From The Edge* was published. It was a satirised version of her drug addiction and strained relationship with her mother, which became a film in 1990. At this point her challenge was to process and deal with this difficult period of her life.

Once she patched things up with Debbie, they grew increasingly close to the point of living next door in a family compound, all of which was shown in a recent poignant documentary called, *Bright Lights.* It actually provides a wonderful demonstration of the empathy and support that "Confluence" can imply.

Now we reach her pivotal age 36 "Year of Revolution" (October, 1992 to October, 1993). Given the negative nature of her mother's own age 36 year, and given she already had her own career and life-defining age 24 "Year of Revolution", with the unprecedented success of *The Empire Strikes Back*, what will we find? There are two very important events in her personal life that happened at this time.

The first is the nature of her short-term relationship with the head of the Creative Artists Agency, Bryan Lourd. This was called a marriage by Carrie at one stage, but there was no formal ceremony. Lourd left Carrie in 1994 (i.e., just past her pivotal age 36 year), for a long-term gay relationship with restaurateur, Bruce Bozzi. She wrote about it in her largely autobiographical follow-up novel *The Best Awful*, in which she says,

> *"I'd had a child with someone who forgot to tell me he was gay. He forgot to tell me and I forgot to notice."*

It had a profound effect on her life and it led to her being an inpatient in a mental facility.

However, her age 36 "Year of Revolution" also largely included the first year of her daughter, Billie, who was born July 17, 1992. They shared almost 9 months of "Confluence", as well as Billie sharing 9 months of "Confluence" with her grandmother. This particular much rarer phenomenon, of more than two closely involved people all sharing some "Confluence" at the time of pivotal events, is what I call a "Whorl of Confluence" and it is the last piece of new terminology I will introduce. I have already included some cases of this in the previous chapter with the main actors in *The Seinfeld Show*, as well as the Google founders, Page and Brin, along with Brin's former wife, Anne.

So it seems, that just as Debbie Reynolds has spoken of her rotten judgement in marrying her three husbands, her daughter Carrie has also followed suit, with her short and tempestuous marriage of nine months to singer Paul Simon, and then her misfortune in her relationship of a couple of years to Bryan Lourd, who left her for a man. So it is not too difficult to imagine how things might have gone in the period October, 1992 to March, 1993, with this "Whorl of Confluence".

Carrie had already written about noticing that things with Lourd were "not quite right" before he announced he was leaving. Meanwhile, Debbie had just opened her ill-fated Las Vegas Hollywood Hotel and named it the Debbie Reynolds Hollywood Hotel. Her wished-for mother/daughter cabaret act was never going to happen.

Carrie was now coping as a first-time mother and her daughter, Billie, was born at a most auspicious time in terms of "Life Cycles Theory". This would be tragically revisited just recently with the sudden deaths of both Carrie and Debbie, during this same "Whorl of Confluence" period.

Of course, their bonds would have been strong, but I would also say that this period would be a particularly important formative influence on Billie's young adult life and career. She wrote recently that, "the prayers and kind words sent to her gave her strength where she thought strength could not exist."

Finally, this period of shared "Confluence" also features her continuing career in the Star Wars movie franchise that made her mother's name. In the 2015 movie *Star Wars VII - The Force Awakens*, Billie takes a cameo role as one her mother's female lieutenants, a character called Kaydel Ko Connix, sporting a similar hairstyle to Princess Leia. Now it transpires Billie has reprised this role in the upcoming *Star Wars VIII* movie to be released at the end of 2017.

She has described how she and her mother were both constantly looking out for each other during the shooting, and how they had a really good time together. Meanwhile, Carrie and Debbie were so close they could be described as inseparable. Yes, this whole example is one of the clearest demonstrations of the amazing shared empathy and support implied by "Confluence".

There is, however, one other amazingly relevant aspect to this saga, this time in terms of the lifelong (and somewhat unlikely) friendship of Debbie Reynolds and the woman who stole her husband, Liz Taylor. Liz, as mentioned previously, was born February 27, 1932, which was an incredible two days before Debbie. This is off-the-scale "Confluence", as it would be predicted, that they would be like two peas in a pod, in terms of friendship.

This is actually just how it turned out in real life. They met as fellow pupils in an MGM school in 1949, which she described as follows, "...she and I were not in any manner alike but we got on very well." Do you remember the same was said about Larry Page and Sergey Brin when they first met?

From thereon they became close friends, in fact so close, that she and Eddie Fisher went on joint holidays with Liz and Mike Todd. Fisher was also Todd's best friend. So when Todd was tragically killed in a plane crash, Fisher was actually encouraged by Reynolds to console Liz, by staying at her house. She had been previously warned by Frank Sinatra, not to marry the much more experienced Fisher, so it would seem that not all was a bed of roses in Debbie's young marriage, in spite of the birth of Carrie in 1956.

However, when Fisher left her for Liz Taylor, it became a huge Hollywood scandal and probably the most talked-about celebrity love triangle of all. I remember on a trip of the city sights of San Francisco, the hotel where they shared some of their assignations was pointed out with pride. Surely this had to be the end of a beautiful friendship because Debbie had been publicly humiliated, both at the time and later when Liz dumped Fisher for the very macho Richard Burton. As most of you know, all of this was front page news back then.

The next chapter was unexpectedly written in 1966, only a relatively short time later, when Debbie, who was now married to her second husband, Harry Karl, happened to be on the same cruise ship as Liz and Richard. Liz sent her a note and Reynolds replied and so the friendship was reignited. They remained close, sharing many happy times, until Liz's death in 2011. Liz always felt guilty about what she had done to her best friend and rather surprisingly bequeathed her some expensive jewellery from her estate.

In fact, somewhat improbably, Carrie also had a strong friendship with Liz, again highlighting the presence of "Confluence". Liz also wanted to atone for the damage she had done to Carrie's upbringing and agreed to star in a 2001 TV movie *These Old Broads*, written and directed by Carrie and starring her mother, Debbie.

The plot had Liz playing a woman who stole the husband of Debbie's character. This is about as close as it gets to real life. Carrie has also said, "if my father had to divorce my mother for anyone, I'm glad that it was Elizabeth…this was a remarkable woman…."

The intricacy of all these elements of "Confluence" in families and friendships is on full display in this one exceptional example. I thought, as I began to write this up, that a fairly simple treatment would suffice, little realising the true wealth of information that it contained. I now want to address the lives of the rest of us relative unknowns, who have equally rich and varied experiences, all of whom I am interested in, but for privacy reasons, most of whom I wouldn't disclose.

I would like to ask, "are you "Confluent" with any other family members or close friends?" If this is the case, then consider the quality of your relationship, particularly at times when you would be in a period of "Confluence". I'm not always looking for examples that are earth-shattering either. For instance, you may remember how I shared almost universal coverage of "Confluence" with both my first supervisor and lifelong friend, from the previous chapter. Well, I have a much more mundane recollection from this time.

After all three of us met up in the one workplace, in our joint age 24/36 "Years of Revolution", there came a time when both my friend and I wanted to leave the organisation some seven years later. Yes, it was another instance of seven years of "Unbroken Forward Momentum" leading on to our combined age 31 "Years of Broken Pathway". By then, both of us were fed up with our supervisor and wanted out. This was a case of too much "Confluence" leading on to getting under each other's skin because the supervisor felt the same way about us.

Well, my friend and I were both interested in one particular opportunity, but he beat me to the punch and left first. So this became his new pathway and uphill challenge at age 31. I stayed on and formally appealed the decision not to award me a senior job that I had held on a temporary basis.

This became my own new pathway and my challenge was to ultimately find a suitable new job, and it was to take a while longer. You know, this is the stuff of everyday lives, but it matters more to me that you may be able to see parallels to this in your own life than to feel that "Life Cycles Theory" and "Confluence" only apply to the famous.

CHAPTER SEVEN

CONFLUENCE AND YOUR WORST ENEMY

Having mentioned several times about the possible negative aspects of "Confluence", I think it is appropriate to illustrate what I am talking about. If almost universal coverage should produce your best friend and confidant, the flip side has to be that if your life circumstances are different, then all that supposed empathy could potentially turn on itself to produce your worst enemy. I am going to the annals of history to study the lives of two of the greatest rivalries from both ancient and modern times.

First back to Ancient Rome, which is one of my favourite periods. I am going to analyse (as best I can allowing for some approximations on dates of birth), the lives of two of the greatest statesman-warriors of this era (or any era for that matter) - Hannibal Barca and his mortal enemy, Scipio Africanus. My attention was first drawn by a number of different sources attesting that they died in the same year, 183 BC. Their ages at death were stated to be 53 for Scipio and 65 for Hannibal, which guarantees they shared "Confluence".

Further investigation revealed a BBC documentary on Hannibal (one of several I have watched), mentioning that when he laid siege to Rome in his only failed attempt, Scipio was said to have been aged 24. Now my best approximation is that this significant and ultimately life-defining event happened during Hannibal's age 36 "Year of Revolution" and this provides still more weight. It will, therefore, become a textbook example of what happens when two individuals, who were so alike, are raised as enemies and make it their life's work to destroy each other.

Both of these men were born into famous military families and were conditioned from an early age, by their equally famous fathers, to pledge allegiance to empires who were sworn enemies. We'll take the elder Hannibal Barca first. He was the son of famous warrior and military leader Hamilcar Barca, who led the Carthaginian Army against Rome in the First Punic War.

When Hannibal was still a child he begged his father to accompany him on one of his military expeditions in modern-day Spain. It is widely reported that during this time Hamilcar held him close to a burning fire and made him swear to "never be a friend of Rome". His father had felt the bitterness of defeat during the First Punic War and had set about striking back at the Roman army, which he had done successfully over the next decade or so, however he died in battle, most probably in 228 BC.

When surrounded by enemy troops, he was said to have thrown himself into the Jucar River in Spain. Thus the unyielding hatred of Rome went even deeper in Hannibal's veins. This traumatic moment could very well have happened when Hannibal was in his age 19 "Year of Broken Pathways". I'd like more certainty with these dates, of course, but the essence of this story will remain regardless.

Let's switch now to the upbringing of young Scipio. He was born into one of Rome's most distinguished families with a record of service in the highest offices stretching back to the early Roman Republic. His father was a noted military commander and Scipio joined him in the army at a young age, before the start of the Second Punic War. Unbelievably, he was said to have made a similar vow to his father that he would "continue the struggle against Carthage all his life."

In short, he was Patrician (i.e., a member of Rome's ruling class) to his bootstraps and was also the son of a famed military father, who had vowed lifelong vengeance on his sworn enemy. I mean, never a greater similarity of two monumental rivals.

Much happened to Hannibal in the years following his father's death. He had become a military commander and when the leader of the Carthaginian army, his brother-in-law Hasdrubal the Fair, was assassinated in 221 BC, Hannibal took over. I'll mention a quote by the Roman historian Livy, regarding his appointment at the time,

> *"no sooner had he arrived...than the old soldiers fancied they saw Hamilcar in his youth given back to them; the same bright look; the same fire in his eye, the same trick of countenance and features. Never was one and the same spirit more skillful to meet opposition, to obey, or to command..."*

So Hannibal was his father incarnate. He was going to be the one who finished his father's business by attacking and destroying Rome itself, in what is known as the Second Punic War. We'll now pick up the threads of when

Hannibal famously crossed the Alps with his army and his elephants, and arrived in what is modern northern Italy. It was Scipio's father who fatefully led the force sent to intercept him. He was surprised to even be fighting Hannibal in this region, because he expected to face the Carthage army in Iberia (Spain).

During what would become the start of the Second Punic War, at the Battle of Trebia in 218 BC, a young Scipio saved his father's life when he was wounded. He bravely rode back into the field of battle to rescue him, even though he was surrounded by enemy horsemen. So here is another pivotal moment between father and son in young adulthood, which was a paramount feature of both lives, as well as illustrating his daring and bravery in battle. The overall Battle of Trebia, however, was decisively won by the Carthage army, being the reverse of the time when Hamilcar was surrounded by Roman troops.

More successful battles followed for Hannibal until the 'big kahuna' in the spring of 216 BC, when he seized the main supply depot for Rome at Cannae. There is good evidence that this occurred in a period of "Confluence" when Hannibal would have been in his age 31 "Year of Broken Pathways", whilst Scipio was most likely in his age 19 year.

The Romans dispatched a huge force in response, but by using brilliant tactics, he managed to totally defeat the much larger Roman army, resulting in estimates of 50-70,000 Romans killed or taken prisoner. It was Rome's most humiliating defeat and it took place in one day. This also affected young Scipio directly, as his future father-in-law died in the battle. Somehow though, Scipio survived this total bloodbath, as well as all the prior battles and, of course, this only intensified his desire to prevail over the Carthage army.

One of the most hotly debated topics between both academics and history buffs in general is whether Hannibal should have taken advantage of Rome's weakened state and immediately attacked the city. The consensus seems to be that he wouldn't have been successful (he lacked effective siege weapons, his soldiers were exhausted and not ready to attack, and he was expecting a Roman surrender anyway); but there are always those like myself, who think it possible, even without directly launching an attack i.e., just by amassing an impressive army outside the walls to instill fear and panic.

If successful, this would have forever changed European history. Hannibal decided to go against the advice of his head of cavalry and took the second city of Capua (just north of modern day Naples) as a base instead. He then continued to ravage the countryside relatively unchecked for the next several years, as the Roman strategy was not to face him in a major battle. Instead, they used guerrilla tactics of skirmishes and pursuing a scorched earth policy (i.e., burning farms and any sources of food), resulting in a strategic stalemate.

If you are well versed in Roman history you may know some or all of this. However here's what you probably don't know. According to legend, after the disastrous Battle of Cannae, Scipio heard that Lucius Caecilius Metellus and other politicians were at the point of surrendering Rome to Hannibal and the Carthaginians. Together with his supporters, he stormed into the meeting and at sword-point he forced all present to swear that they would continue in faithful service to Rome. Fortunately, the Roman Senate was of like mind and refused to entertain thoughts of peace, despite the great losses Rome had taken in the war. Approximately one-fifth of the men of military age had died within a few years of Hannibal's invasion.

So it may have boiled down to a simple battle of wills in the end. If this was true (and I suspect it might be), then Hannibal never even knew what an opportunity he missed. His bitter rival, however, 19-year-old Scipio, showing incredible nerve for his age, knew exactly what Hannibal could potentially do and sealed his fate with his daring actions. Never a better illustration of "Confluence" between close rivals, in this case resulting in their mutual fates being sealed in their combined "Years of Broken Pathway".

Now this builds up to their next combined significant year when Scipio would be in his age 24 "Year of Revolution", at the same time as Hannibal was in his important and often career-defining age 36 "Year of Revolution". What is going to happen to them both that will markedly affect their futures? That will, in a sense, again mutually seal their fates?

For Hannibal, relations with Rome in his important age 36 year (i.e., part of 212 BC and 211 BC), had amounted to a strategic stalemate. Roman forces gathered outside his Capua headquarters every time he was away, but they retreated when he promptly returned. He really wanted to meet the Roman army head-on in battle and defeat them, however they weren't having any of it. So in the summer of 211 BC, he decided to lay siege to Rome itself, in order to draw them into the open.

He camped outside the Roman city walls for the first and only time in his life. This, unfortunately, was not on his terms. It wasn't a true siege, for he lacked effective weapons and supplies for a lengthy encounter and planned it only as a feint. Not nearly the same as it would have been after the devastating Battle of Cannae with the Roman army decimated. In 216 BC, with or without siege weapons, he would have created wholesale panic and exerted much psychological pressure.

Now some five years later it was reported that Roman Patricians, far from being frightened, were openly selling the land he occupied for real estate purposes. Can you imagine this? They were making a mockery of him. One thing the last five years had taught them was resolve and patience to wait this warrior out. Word of his ineffective siege got back to the besiegers of Capua and they simply continued. On hearing this Hannibal had to retreat back to the south and Capua fell to the Roman forces soon after.

So for Hannibal, his central and often life and career-defining age of 36 did not contain a magnificent victory, only a humiliating defeat and with it the loss of much prestige throughout the whole region. Cities that had defected to him after Cannae, were switching back their allegiance to Rome. He no longer had Capua as his home base and the Romans knew that, and from this point onwards they had the upper hand. He would now be the one pursued, rather than the pursuer. This unfortunate turn of events was to set in train a pattern of repetition throughout the rest of his life. He would continue to be persecuted by Rome, in one form or another, until his death many years later.

Now let's switch to Scipio. His age 24 "Year of Revolution" contained a major setback, that preceded a bold endeavour, which defined the rest of his life. He was the veritable definition of "Life Cycles Theory" in action. Firstly, tragedy struck his family in 211 BC, when both his father Publius Scipio and his uncle Gnaeus Cornelius Scipio Calvus were killed in battle in Hispania (Spain) by Hannibal's brother, Hasdrubal. At the election of a new Proconsul for an army to be sent to Spain, only one candidate put himself forward to the Senate for consideration - Scipio.

The reason for this was because it was regarded as a virtual death sentence by others, but Scipio wanted to avenge his family's honor, even more than the risks incurred. Again, in spite of his youth, his demeanour and enthusiastic language made so great an impression that he was elected unanimously. So his crowning achievement was to become a General and a Proconsul, and to go after Hannibal's family, who were responsible for the deaths of his father and uncle.

This was to be stage one in his personal war with Hannibal. Not a showdown just yet, more a platform to begin his ultimate quest. This leads us to their next shared period of "Confluence" because now their paths were narrowing. Some seven years later we have their combined "Years of Broken Pathway" (at age 43 for Hannibal and age 31 for Scipio), which amounted to a shared period in the years 205 BC and mostly 204 BC.

It is stated by Roman historian Livy, that Scipio was made a Full Consul in 205 BC at the age of 31, due to his over-riding success in driving Carthaginian forces out of Spain over the last several years. Now his goal was set, to invade Africa and defeat Hannibal in battle once and for all. In spite of only limited support and a small number of troops and cavalry, he set sail from Sicily to the African coast in 204 BC. His immediate attempt to take the city of Utica was unsuccessful, so he now had to dig in for winter and wait. In this case his challenge was clear, how to use superior tactics against much larger enemy forces. This was very similar to what Hannibal had done himself at Cannae, some 12 years earlier.

Meanwhile, at the same time, Hannibal was just about a spent force in the southern Roman countryside. He was reduced to fighting a guerrilla-style war from his hideout in the mountains. Roman armies sent to get rid of him met with only mixed success, but it was Scipio who once again knew the right tactics. He convinced a sceptical Senate to send him to Africa with a tiny force, knowing the powers that be in Carthage would call Hannibal back. This is precisely what they did very soon after and it defined Hannibal's uphill challenge. So again, these mortal enemies drew closer to meeting, as a result of their actions in this combined "Significant Year".

In the battle of Zama, in 202 BC, Scipio's outnumbered forces finally defeated Hannibal by using some of his own tactics from Cannae against him. This closed the 17-year-long Second Punic War, but what interests me is that it also marked the first time these two great military leaders met. This was organised before the battle to discuss Hannibal's proposal to give up overseas territories, but retain sovereign control of Carthage. Scipio refused saying it was total surrender or war. Hannibal said, "what you are today, I was back at Cannae." He also said that it was the fates that decided our lives, as there are so many things outside our control that influence the outcome.

This was a very apt description of "Life Cycles Theory". He was describing how the tables had turned completely in 12 years, since they were last in a decisive and direction-changing "Year of Broken Pathways". Being the elder and reflecting back, he was able to see how neither man had ultimate control of his destiny. He was even able to say, that both had almost no choice in doing what they did, because of their circumstances of birth. However, it was not his time and he lost the battle, surrendered and never again led a Carthage army.

There is one important post-script for this story and it was in the autumn of 193 BC (when Scipio was in his age 43 "Year of Broken Pathways" and Hannibal was most probably in his age 55 "Year of Broken Pathways"). This has become a legendary final meeting between the two mighty generals. It took place in the court of Antiochus III of Syria, where Hannibal was advising the Syrians how to conduct a war with Rome. Scipio was sent to settle the differences rather than resort to battle. The two met at dinner and Scipio asked Hannibal who he considered the greatest general of all (no doubt looking for some flattery).

Hannibal named Alexander The Great as the first and Pyrrhus the second, because of his tactical skills. He then said he was third. At this Scipio broke into a sardonic laugh and said, "what would you say if you had beaten me?" Hannibal replied that beyond doubt he would have put himself first. This amounted to a back-handed compliment to Scipio, but not what he wanted to hear. This witticism became the final salvo in the Punic War, since it was reported to have deeply troubled Scipio afterward.

However, against all odds, the bonds between these two warrior-statesmen began to run deep. When Scipio retired in acrimonious circumstances, after allegations of bribery of Antiochus, he fought with Rome over trying to prevent the ruin of the exiled Hannibal. His great magnanimity showed the positive aspects of "Confluence" in a story so strange, it is almost impossible to conceive. Finally, both men died in the same year, as embittered and estranged from their homelands. Hannibal in exile, while the inscription on Scipio's tomb showed just how he felt. It read, "ungrateful fatherland, you will not even have my bones."

The next famous historical example of "Confluence" between rivals and enemies also came to me by accident. A couple of years ago I wrote about the profiles of the two contestants for Australian Prime Minister in the 2013 general elections. They didn't like each other, they were born in the same year and had almost universal coverage for "Confluence".

The incumbent, a man of considerable ego, had resuscitated his career and was said to be like Napoleon coming back from Elba. His opponent, who was plain spoken and a man of spartan physical habits, was admonished to find his 'inner Duke of Wellington' (as most readers know, this was the man who defeated Napoleon in his last battle at Waterloo). Interesting I thought, and then I checked and found out these two famous historical leaders were also born in the same year!

Yes, Napoleon Bonaparte was born August 15, 1769 and Arthur Wellesley (the future Duke of Wellington) was born May 1, 1769, meaning they shared around 8½ months of "Confluence" for every "Significant Year". This example, however, is in no way a lifelong merging of circumstances and personalities, for they didn't really cross swords until close to their momentous battle.

Both were first and foremost military men, who began their careers early on and achieved significant promotions in their first shared age 24 "Year of Revolution". In the case of Napoleon, he found a way to successfully end the pivotal Siege of Toulon. He began as an artillery major, but after the victory he won acclaim in Paris, being promoted to Brigadier-General, as I have previously mentioned. His victory was preceded by an initial failure, due to the ineptness of the local commanders, who Napoleon petitioned to be replaced. So here is another example of a "Moment of Setback/Frustration" before the eventual breakthrough.

With Arthur Wellesley, his "Moment of Setback/Frustration" was his rejection as a suitor to marry an aristocratic girl, because of his debts and poor prospects. This determined him to succeed in the military. He became a major by purchase and a few months later in September, 1793 (i.e., in his age 24 "Year of Revolution", which was May, 1793 to May, 1794), he was loaned money by his brother to purchase a lieutenant-colonelcy. He then took command of a British regiment and sailed to Flanders for his first battle. This amounted to his first adult career identity.

I remind readers, that though I knew about the Siege of Toulon because I wrote about it in Book Two, I literally discovered the Arthur Wellesley story at the same time as I was writing about it. It was exactly the same with Book Two when I had a hypothesis first, before I got the proof on Napoleon. Some well-intentioned comments by psychiatrists and psychologists I know, suggest that my hypotheses are a normal enough phase of early adult life when you could expect these things, but I reiterate to them and to you, "why do I not find them as occurring just randomly in any year of the decade of your 20s, but rather as a tightly-defined formula in just one year?" I have case after case after case of this, so relatively mundane to me now, that only the odd exception draws my interest.

Rolling forward to the career and life-defining age 36 "Year of Revolution" for both men, we'll first look at one of my most often quoted cases, that of Napoleon's success at the Battle of Austerlitz. He managed to defeat the combined armies of the Austrian and Russian Empires in one day to effectively gain control of Europe, and he is on record as saying it was the thing he is most proud of in his life. This was preceded by the disastrous Battle of Trafalgar, only seven weeks prior, where he lost two-thirds of his combined French-Spanish fleet to Horatio Nelson.

Arthur Wellesley had an altogether different age 36 "Year of Revolution". After a long and successful career in India, rising to the rank of Major-General, he stated in 1804 that, "I have served as long in India as any man ought, who can serve somewhere else." He was made a Knight of the Bath and now had amassed a fortune of 42,000 pounds from prize money in his campaigns. So in March, 1805, he and his brother (who had served as Governor-General of India) sailed back to England.

It is of passing interest that during their journey (which could well be around the start of Arthur's age 36 year on May 1, 1805), they briefly stayed at the little island of St. Helena and slept in the very same building to which Napoleon would be exiled. However, that was in the future and right now things were not going well for Britain or her Allies in Europe. Wellesley was sent to North Germany as part of an abortive Anglo-Russian campaign that achieved very little and was recalled to England. This amounted to his "Moment of Frustration/Setback", as he'd had enough of the military and took extended leave. He re-emerged soon after, when he was elected Tory member for Rye in January, 1806, and went on to become Chief Secretary to Ireland, which became his "Moment of Breakthrough/Achievement".

This was to ultimately become his new age/direction, as he was to serve two terms as Prime Minister of the United Kingdom and be distinguished for service as Home Secretary, Foreign Secretary and Secretary of State for War and the Colonies. It is as a statesman that he achieved the hallmark of his career.

You'd think that would be enough change for one year, but there was one more fascinating development in his personal life, which also came to define his destiny. With his new-found wealth and prestige, he decided to look up

Kitty Pakenham, who was his former would-be wife of some twelve years prior.

She was still single and had broken off an engagement because a female friend told her Wellesley still wanted her. This had affected her health and when they finally met Wellesley remarked to his brother, "she has grown ugly by Jove!" Nonetheless the wedding went ahead in April, 1806 (still within the age 36 year) and they stayed married until her death, although they lived separately for many years. They finally reconciled their personal differences on her deathbed, in a tragic tale of an unfulfilled love story.

The path between our second set of mortal enemies is about to narrow at their next shared "Significant Year" when they were both in their age 43 "Year of Broken Pathways". For Napoleon, the winter of the year 1812 represented the greatest direction change and challenge I have ever analysed, as he lost around 90% of his Grand Armee during the failed Russian Invasion and was now very much in decline all around Europe.

Wellesley had decided to rejoin the military and in 1808, he sailed to Portugal to take part in what was known as the Peninsula Campaign. As a Lieutenant-General he commanded a force of 9,000 men. This was a long and arduous campaign, that stretched over a number of years. In July, 1812 (when he was in his age 43 year) he distinguished himself by overwhelming French forces at the Battle of Salamanca and liberating Madrid as a result. He was then created an Earl and shortly after that, Marquess of Wellington, and now had control of all Allied armies in Spain.

His main adversary was Napoleon's brother Joseph, who had the title King of Spain. Napoleon was counting on Joseph to maintain control, but his "Year of Broken Pathways" was all about a direction change to being in retreat. It proved no different in Spain when Wellington smashed Joseph's army in the Battle of Vitoria in June, 1813 (still within Napoleon's age 43 year). For this he was hailed a hero, created a Field Marshall and became the Duke of Wellington. Never a more radical difference in fortunes in their shared "Years of Broken Pathways" for these deadly rivals.

Finally, their last shared age 48 "Year of Revolution" (August, 1817 to May, 1818), contains a couple of fascinating stories. You would think that once Napoleon was safely in custody on the remote St. Helena Island and Wellington was effectively in control of France during the re-establishment of the monarchy, things would be relatively uneventful. But there was never an uneventful time in the tumultuous life of Emperor Napoleon.

As long as Napoleon lived, the possibility of escape to either Europe or North or South America, occupied the minds of all his old officers and followers, many of whom had sought asylum in different parts of the New World. In July, 1817, a letter (known as the Philadelphia Letter), alluding to escape plans by two fast sailing boats, was intercepted by the British secret service. Whilst Wellington wasn't part of this development (Lord Bathurst was responsible for Napoleon as Secretary of War and the Colonies), he would have been privy to all matters regarding his rival, as the plotters first option was to take Napoleon to France.

The escape attempt was expected to happen in February, 1818, but one of the chief conspirators, a Colonel Lapatie, was arrested and deported from Brazil. This and other reported attempts make for fascinating reading, however I don't have time to get distracted from the main story. Napoleon was fully aware of these plots, which were orchestrated by his brother, Joseph, who was living in the US. Undoubtedly, his "Year of Revolution" was about seeing this intrigue come to nothing, and having to accommodate to a life in seclusion and to writing his memoirs.

So, no direct intersect with Wellington, but both men were well-informed about each other. Wellington's "Year of Revolution" had one dramatic moment that could be termed a "Moment of Setback/Frustration" and that was an assassination attempt in Paris in February, 1818. He was fired upon, but otherwise unharmed and though there were also many plotters out to kill him, he steadfastly went about his daily routine (as you would expect of someone called the 'Iron Duke').

Thus, at the same time as Napoleon could have been rescued from St. Helena and potentially get back to France, Wellington could have been assassinated. Neither of these unlikely scenarios occurred. Wellington continued to distinguish himself by maintaining good discipline over the 120,000 troops placed all around France, and dealing with the possibility of an uprising of disgruntled locals. It was onwards and upwards for him, as he returned to England soon after and resumed his political career, rising to Prime Minister in 1828.

Another interesting corner in this great historical story was that some concern was shown by Wellington for the overly strict conditions under which Napoleon had to live on St. Helena. These included being denied firewood and having to burn his own furniture to keep warm during winter, as well as sell Imperial silverware to pay for his accommodation.

His gaoler, General Hudson Lowe, was too zealous in carrying out his orders and this created a storm of criticism in both Europe and England, forcing him to withdraw these measures. Wellington, a man of strict discipline himself, said of Lowe,

> *"a very bad choice; he was a man wanting in education and judgment. He was a stupid man, he knew nothing at all of the world, and like all men who knew nothing of the world, he was suspicious and jealous."*

This concludes my journey through some forgotten corners of very famous historical stories. It is now time to get right into a few nitty-gritty modern casework studies of "Confluence", so for those of you wanting to get the lowdown on some current romantic dilemmas, of the sort written about in gossip magazines, this is your time. Mind you, the moment I think I've got a reasonable handle on very recent celebrity affairs, some new development seems to pop up. Nonetheless I'll do my best to report as accurately as I can.

CHAPTER EIGHT

CONFLUENCE AND CURRENT AFFAIRS

There is a great fascination in certain affairs of the heart that are played out on the public stage, but probably none more so than the famous love triangle involving Brad Pitt, his former wife Jennifer Aniston, and his current estranged and about to be divorced wife, Angelina Jolie. Because just about everyone knows about it, this makes it ideal for my purposes. My data can be readily checked by anyone.

William Bradley Pitt was born December 18, 1963, and came to notice in his age 24 "Year of Revolution" (December, 1987 to December, 1988), with his first leading film role in *Dark Side Of The Sun*, which was about the Croatian War of Independence. After a period of seven years of "Unbroken Forward Momentum", where he mostly played rather lightweight, 'pretty-boy' roles, he finally achieved both critical and commercial success with the hit movie *Seven*, when he was in his age 31 "Year of Broken Pathways".

That was a very brief career summary in terms of "Life Cycles Theory", but we now need to examine his love life. After dating a string of actress co-stars, he met Gwyneth Paltrow during the making of *Seven* and had a relationship of a couple of years. It should be noted that there was no "Confluence" between them, even though they became engaged in 1998 and many thought they would marry. It appeared Brad got cold feet, as he called off the wedding plans abruptly. This all took place when Paltrow was in her own age 24 "Year of Revolution" and was very unsettling for her.

In the next year, Pitt met *Friends'* star Jennifer Aniston, who was born February 11, 1969, meaning they shared around 10 out of a possible 12 months of "Confluence" in every second "Significant Year". If you remember my definitions from an earlier chapter, this would give them a large amount of "Partial Confluence". The culmination of their romance led on to marriage in a private ceremony on July 29, 2000. This coincided with one of their "Window of Opportunity" periods, when Brad would have been in his important age 36 "Year of Revolution" and Jennifer would have been in her age 31 "Year of

Broken Pathways" (February to December, 2000). At this time they were America's golden couple and after several years together were celebrated as an outstanding example of two stars finding lasting love in the often fickle world of Hollywood.

They were also an outstanding example of how two people, who were quite "Confluent", combined love and friendship and were talking about starting a family. Pitt's quote before the filming of *Mr. And Mrs. Smith* was, "I'm happier now than I have ever been." So where did it all go wrong and more importantly in terms of this chapter, did it have anything to do with "Confluence"? The answer for me, as always, is in the analysis.

Angelina Jolie was born June 4, 1975, meaning that she shared some 5½ months of "Confluence" with Pitt for every shared "Significant Year". This was a clear case of "Full Confluence" with Jolie, versus "Partial Confluence" with Aniston. Now my basic principle for "Confluence" is the more the better, although compatibility is not necessarily guaranteed and such relationships can only be studied retrospectively.

The movie *Mr. And Mrs. Smith* (2005), began the real-life romance of Jolie and the then-married Pitt. This caused a great scandal, like the Taylor-Burton romance did during *Cleopatra*. Aniston, who was the injured party in all of this, happened to be in her all-important age 36 "Year of Revolution" when their separation was announced and followed fairly quickly by a divorce, finalised in September, 2005.

In a memoir covering this period, the person who introduced Pitt and Jolie said that, "he fell in love with her during the production" and that, "he immediately sensed there was a spark between them." This chemistry is something that can't always be rationally controlled or explained and as I have previously stated, can surface at inappropriate moments.

It is interesting from my perspective to note that neither Pitt nor Jolie were in a "Significant Year" when this occurred. He was then 41 and she was 29. This was not therefore in a "Window of Opportunity" period, like it was for say, Chaplin and O'Neill, or Bogie and Bacall, or Juan and Eva. No, this love story was built on the unfortunate foundation of Jennifer Aniston's angst, in her life-changing age 36 "Year of Revolution". Though many fans would have liked to see Brad and Jen reunite and perhaps some do even now, it would seem that the die has been cast.

Let's now project forward to the only "Window of Opportunity" period for Pitt and Jolie, when he was aged 48 and she was aged 36 (i.e., December, 2011 to June, 2012). Were there any developments in their relationship? This period coincided with an announcement of their engagement in April, 2012, when she showed off her $1 million engagement ring. Pitt's manager said, "Yes, it's confirmed. It's a promise for the future and their kids are very happy. There's no date set at this time." Although the actual marriage was not till 2014, the first public announcement of their intentions happened in Jolie's important age 36 year.

It should also be noted that in terms of her career, her age 36 "Year of Revolution" (June, 2011 to June, 2012) coincided with the release of the movie *In The Land Of Blood And Honey*, in December, 2011. This was her directorial debut and was a graphic account of a love story set in the 1992-1995 Bosnian war. It was nominated for a Golden Globe for Best Foreign Language Film and she was given honorary citizenship of Sarajevo for raising awareness of the war. As a personal high point for a decade of humanitarian work, in April, 2012, she was promoted to the role of Special Envoy for the United Nations High Commission for Refugees. So, at the very time that she and Pitt announced their engagement, she received this well-publicised personal honour. This is a great example of a dual "Moment of Breakthrough/ Achievement" if ever there was one. So, chalk up just one more black and white example of "Life Cycles Theory" in action.

This whole period must also be seen in terms of the other protagonist in the former love triangle, Jennifer Aniston. After a period of some seven years of "Unbroken Forward Momentum", since her shock divorce in 2005, she also had some good news of her own to share with the world. She and her new partner, Justin Theroux, announced their engagement in August, 2012, when Jennifer was midway through her own age 43 "Year of Broken Pathways". In fact, events in this year corresponded perfectly with "Life Cycles Theory", which says your new direction in a "Year of Broken Pathways" often sneaks up on you bit by bit. Here is her timeline for 2012.

On February 22, right at the start of this direction-altering year, she received her star on Hollywood's Walk of Fame. To celebrate the moment, she gave Theroux a kiss on the lips, which was their first public display of affection since they began dating a couple of years ago. Then, in April, a gossip magazine erroneously stated they were planning to get married in Crete. She denied there were any plans to marry.

However, things began to heat up in June, when the couple shared a romantic holiday in Paris and were then photographed aboard a rented yacht in Capri, Italy. The quote was, "he makes her feel safe and secure when she's with him." Then on August 8, a magazine again wrongly claimed they had split up, because of Theroux's unwillingness to commit. More denials had to be issued. Finally, only two days later, on Theroux's birthday, he popped the question. Reporters noted that Pitt and Jolie's engagement was only a short time ago.

You should note the exquisite timing in terms of "Life Cycles Theory". At 31, Jennifer marries Brad in a romantic ceremony. At 36, Jennifer's life is torn apart, when she separates and divorces Brad after he meets and falls in love with Jolie. Now, at 43, she finally announces her engagement to Theroux, after a romantic European holiday. Others mentioned the 12-year span in these developments. It's, of course, only a passing comment for them, but for me it's much, much more. The same as it was for the Burton-Taylor relationship.

Once again, did I know all this before I began to write it up? To be honest, I knew about the marriage to Brad and then the divorce, but that's it. No particular knowledge of career high points or engagements. That's why I know the really honest response to my theory is from ordinary, open-minded people, who simply say to me, "gee, that's just spooky!" It is, you know, and it doesn't need intellectualising and rationalising or trying to explain in terms of your own predilections. It's, well, just plain spooky.

I began with the idea of writing about this wonderfully "Confluent" couple with the nickname Brangelina, but events overtook me and the seemingly happily-ever-after couple, with a tribe of kids, suddenly became one the world's messiest pending divorces. How would I deal with this? It's simply real life and I have absolutely no control over what happens, any more than anyone else. A perfect example of not all major events neatly fitting into my "Significant Years" and a good foil for my last idle moment of self-congratulation. So, let's see what we have here? One of the catalysts for this next section was Jolie's well-reported fit of jealousy over Pitt's relationship with his new leading lady, the well-known French actress, Marion Cotillard.

I don't know why, but I decided to look at Cotillard's birth data. Then it jumped out at me. She was born September 30, 1975. That makes her some 4 months younger than Jolie, which means her and Pitt share even more "Confluence", at 9½ months compared to 5½ months. Again the principle of the more the better, all things being equal, should mean that she and Brad should hit it off famously when they acted together as husband and wife in the

WWII spy movie *Allied*.

There is no question that Marion and Brad shared some amazing chemistry on set and that it certainly got other cast and crew talking about whether something may be going on between them. A magazine quote stated, "they had insane chemistry from the start and many crew members believe they've been acting on it in private...they have affectionate nicknames for each other and she lights up whenever he is on set." Angie was said to have turned up to check out for herself what was happening.

Here we have a further dramatic example of the instant chemistry that can occur when two people, who are strongly "Confluent", meet up. It can be fine and dandy, if they are each without other primary relationships, but damned inconvenient if they are, say, both married and fully committed elsewhere. Reporters were quick to point out the irony of the situation, which was that almost exactly 12 years ago it was Angie, who played a married spy in the movie *Mr. And Mrs. Smith,* and it resulted in a scandalous divorce from Brad's then wife Jennifer. They similarly had flatly denied any off-screen romance.

Now Marion is not a replay of Angelina and she has said she is happily married and pregnant with her second child to her husband, although the timing gave rise to scurrilous speculations. My real interest again is the simple, well-stated fact, that the Pitt-Jolie relationship lasted for 12 years. OK, not at a "Significant Year", but we have another 12-year interval, just as we did with the Aniston-Pitt-Theroux 12-year journey, from marriage to divorce to a new engagement.

A final and oddball postscript is that neither Aniston and Theroux nor Cotillard and her husband Guillaume Canet share any "Confluence". Neither do the reported new partners for Pitt and Jolie. I don't want to become as bad as the gossip mags, so I'll leave out the names, but you can check it out easily for yourselves at any newsstand. So, not every love story involving "Confluence" has a happy end, but then again Camelot, as the song goes, only existed for one brief shining moment.

Just before completion, I have now seen confirmation that Aniston and Theroux have separated, "on an amicable basis around Christmas, 2017". This new twist has therefore happened within Aniston's age 48 "Year of Revolution", so in her case it's a direct rerun of her separation and divorce from Brad 12 years earlier at 36. This, in turn, has sparked unfounded rumours of her getting back together with Brad, so it is becoming a long running saga indeed.

This is now displayed graphically for you on the next page.

GWYNETH PALTROW
"No Partial Confluence"

DOB: 27.09.1972

JENNIFER ANISTON
10 months
"Partial Confluence"

DOB: 11.02.1969

BRAD PITT

DOB: 18.12.1963

ANGELINA JOLIE
5 ½ months
"Full Confluence"

DOB: 04.06.1975

MARION COTILLARD
9 ½ months
"Full Confluence"

DOB: 30.09.1975

Let's now examine the marriages of a well-known star, where he shared around the same amount of "Confluence" with all three of his wives. The person concerned is Tom Cruise. Tom was born July 3, 1962, and his first marriage was to the actress Mimi Rogers, who was born January 27, 1956, which meant they shared 5 months of "Partial Confluence" in every second "Significant Year".

The first instance of this occurring was the period January to July, 1987, when Cruise would have been in his age 24 "Year of Revolution" and Rogers would have been in her age 31 "Year of Broken Pathways". This was in a "Window of Opportunity" period for them, when their marriage happened in May, 1987. Just prior to this happening Cruise, while still in his age 24 "Year of Revolution", was introduced by Rogers to her religion of Scientology.

This has so far proved to be the beginning of his lifelong association with the controversial group. Rogers' father was a friend of L. Ron Hubbard and she was a highly trained auditor with the church. Naturally, she would introduce a younger Cruise before they were married. There was another issue for her, however, which was that her father had become estranged from mainstream Scientology. It was assumed by leader David Miscavige, that his daughter might go the same way.

These misgivings, according to an extensive article in *The Sydney Morning Herald*, prompted Miscavige to seek to undermine their marriage. According to Marty Rathbun, an ex-senior Scientology member, there were active plans to encourage Cruise's attraction to Nicole Kidman on the set of *Days Of Thunder*. This was successful, because the outcome was they fell in love and Cruise's marriage to Rogers was soon over. Nicole's relationship with Tom lasted 12 years from meeting in 1989 to divorce in 2001, similarly to the Pitt-Jolie and Burton-Taylor relationships.

Because of Nicole's own star power, this became a high-profile marriage. Nicole Kidman was born June 20, 1967, so again they shared "Partial Confluence", but this time for a much longer period, almost 12 months for every second "Significant Year". During their relationship there was only one instance of a period of "Confluence", which was from July, 1998 to June, 1999, when Tom was in his important age 36 "Year of Revolution", while Nicole was in her direction altering, age 31 "Year of Broken Pathways". The big question for me becomes, "what, if anything, took place in that time?"

This bedevilled me for some while, until the answer came jumping out from left-field. Once again it was tied up with Scientology and how it related to Nicole as an approved-of partner. She was the daughter of a well-known psychologist and Scientology had a problem with psychology and psychiatry. So Miscavige seemed to have, in effect, swapped one problem wife with another. She was also born and raised a Catholic and despite an earlier, apparently sincere, foray into becoming a Scientologist, she had lost interest over a number of years.

It was in 1997, during the filming of *Eyes Wide Shut*, that she publicly announced she was no longer a Scientologist. This had affected Cruise at the time, who adored his wife and was also drifting away. This critical period saw Cruise not returning Miscavige's phone calls. It was reported by Rathbun, that a Michael Doven had been instructed to bring him back into the fold and that in October, 1998 (right in their "Window of Opportunity" period) he began almost continuous auditing sessions with Cruise. The prime goal, states Rathbun, was, "to keep planting a seed and to drive a wedge between Tom and Nicole."

This finally bore fruit a couple of years later in their shock 2001 divorce. Nicole was blindsided by this and Cruise's only comment on the reason was, "Ask Nic, she knows." So, when Cruise was 36, he had it put squarely to him that he needed to get back to Scientology, even if it cost him his marriage. For Nicole, her age 31 "Year of Broken Pathways" was coming to the gradual realisation about what might be happening in these auditing sessions, and facing the uphill challenge of the impact on her family life.

It was also an interesting development for me when I looked at Nicole's second marriage to well-known country musician and fellow Australian, Keith Urban. Keith was indeed born only 4 months later than Nicole, on October 26, 1967. This gives them "Full Confluence" covering 8 out of a possible 12 months for every shared "Significant Year". By the more the better principle for "Confluence", this would mark them as even more closely suited both in romance and friendship, than Nicole was with Tom.

Their wonderful 10-year marriage and family of two girls bears a testament to this, even though when they were in their recent combined age 48 "Years of Revolution" (i.e., October, 2015 to June, 2016), there were a number of rumours circulating about marriage difficulties. Whatever these details may have amounted to, they currently seem to have well and truly been dealt with. But our focus is Tom's marriages and we must now return to his renewed quest for love after his second divorce in 2001.

You'd have thought that the church would have very closely vetted his next choice, which was Katie Holmes, but they appeared to let her strong Catholic upbringing pass. Katie was born December 18, 1978, meaning that once again she shared around 5½ months of "Partial Confluence". This was very close to the amount in the Mimi Rogers relationship and about half as much as the Kidman relationship.

Similarly to Tom and Nicole, she and Tom shared only one "Window of

Opportunity" period and that was between July and December, 2010, when Tom was in his age 48 "Year of Revolution" and Katie was in her age 43 "Year of Broken Pathways". This sets up a fascinating hypothesis. We know they were divorced not long after this, so did this period again feature marriage difficulties and did it have reference to Katie, as an approved-of wife within Scientology?

Now I'd like to be able to show more publicly verifiable data than I am able to, so I'll be forced to examine reports immediately prior to and towards the end of this time and base my rough conclusions on it. Similarly to Nicole, Katie began studying Scientology in the early stages of their relationship and seemed to be going down the right path when they were married in 2006.

However it was reported, that once she became a member, she did not necessarily like the new lifestyle. This became manifest in October, 2009, when it was widely reported that her daughter, Suri, would be attending a Catholic pre-school. This was apparently preceded by strong arguments with Tom, who naturally wanted a Scientology option.

There is no doubt it would have sent up a red flag with Scientology headquarters, because it could have signalled a rerun of what happened with Nicole. Then there was a brief report in a Hollywood magazine dated November, 2010, talking about a rough patch in their marriage and differences of opinion in raising their daughter. They were reported to be, in effect, living separate lives at this time.

Rather than wait for the church to persuade Tom to dissociate himself from her, Katie decided to learn from Nicole's blindsiding and instigated a quick divorce in 2012, while also winning custody rights for her daughter. In all of this saga what we are seeing is strong evidence of a continuing theme running throughout Tom's life at every one of his adult "Years of Revolution".

So at 24 he becomes a Scientologist, when he meets and marries Mimi Rogers, who has grown up in the church. Then at 36, there is a crisis over wife number two, Nicole Kidman, potentially luring him away from Scientology. The church goes all out to drive a wedge between them and gets him to return to the fold. Finally, at 48, there appears to be another crisis over wife number three, Katie Holmes, wanting their daughter to be raised as a Catholic and creating more of the same issues for the church to deal with.

The obvious continuation of this theme, with a different wife at every one of his adult "Years of Revolution", is the essence of "Life Cycles Theory". I always look for the common link in the behavioural patterns and when it stands out like this I call it "Substantive Similarity", as opposed to a more underlying "Symbolic Similarity". Here, for the first time, I have illustrated how periods of "Confluence" even between different partners can represent the same storyline.

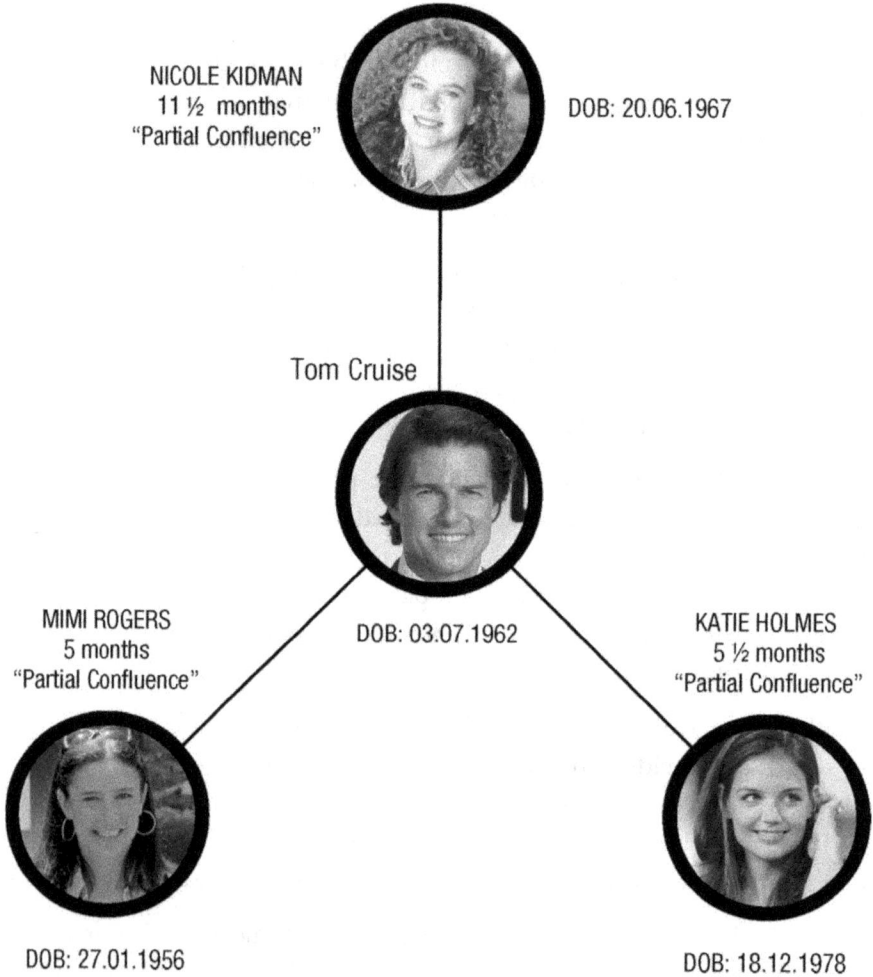

NICOLE KIDMAN
11 ½ months
"Partial Confluence"

DOB: 20.06.1967

Tom Cruise

DOB: 03.07.1962

MIMI ROGERS
5 months
"Partial Confluence"

KATIE HOLMES
5 ½ months
"Partial Confluence"

DOB: 27.01.1956

DOB: 18.12.1978

I must say, I have done exactly the same thing with the various wives and partners of the always popular John Cleese. Not only did all these women share a similar amount of "Confluence" with John, but in a couple of cases it boiled down to being born in the same year. Further than this, they were all physically and demographically similar, being blonde American actors and artists, who are usually into psychology and counselling as well. Their almost predictable relationship breakdowns had a similarity with regard to

"Confluence". It's a fascinating story and though I didn't intend to write about it, once I started this narrative, again it overtook me. Those who have read Book Two will observe how this phenomenon happened to my material in a similar section of that book.

John appears to have a four-step process in his love life. Step one is to fall madly in love and get married more or less at once. Step two is to have some sort of disagreement/clash of values and try to sort it out with counselling. Step three then becomes, after that doesn't work, start to live separate lives under the one roof. Finally, step four is to separate and get divorced amicably with a reasonable settlement.

Let's now start our investigation. His first and best-known wife was actress/writer turned psychologist, Connie Booth. Connie was born on January 31, 1944, while John Cleese was born October 27, 1939, meaning they shared three months of "Partial Confluence" for every second "Significant Year". She was the daughter of a Wall Street magnate, whose mother persuaded her to go into acting.

She met Cleese when she was 20 and he was in his age 24 "Year of Revolution" and the attraction was instant. They were both feisty and he liked her ability to express herself. She became a controlling influence in their marriage and she was a lot closer to the character 'Sybil' (which she co-wrote) than to 'Polly the Maid' (which she played). Coincidentally, when Cleese was aged 24, he also hit the big time when the *Cambridge Revue* (that he was a member of), got onto Broadway and the *Ed Sullivan Show*. That was why he was in New York and met Connie.

They were married a little later in her own age 24 "Year of Revolution" and it lasted effectively for seven years, so again we see this same period of "Unbroken Forward Momentum". When Cleese was in his age 31 "Year of Broken Pathways", he and Connie accidentally met Donald Sinclair at the hotel Gleneagles, where they were staying. Sinclair was the real-life Basil Fawlty and it was to eventually lead on to their hit show *Fawlty Towers*, which was launched when Cleese was in his all-important age 36 "Year of Revolution". Yet another landmark piece of evidence.

That is not the focus of our current investigation, however. What we are here to analyse is the only period of shared "Confluence" between John and Connie, that occurred in the period October, 1975 to January, 1976, when they would have been aged 36 and 31 respectively. We also need to understand that leading up to this, they both got into therapy individually.

In 1973, Cleese turned up at a doctor's office saying he had the 'flu, but instead was told he was suffering from depression. You can almost see this real-life drama as a Monty Python sketch. Connie grew up with dysfunctional parents, whose screaming matches caused the police to be called. It is little wonder then that their marriage was beginning to crumble around them, even without any third parties being involved.

In 1974, while co-writing Fawlty, they lived separately under one roof. They tried marriage counselling, but in late 1975 or early 1976, they formally separated, with the divorce happening in 1978. This appears to correlate exactly with their only "Window of Opportunity" period. I have found other cases of estranged couples separating rather than reconciling, in a seeming reversal of what might be expected. Her settlement on divorce was a fairly small sum and they remain friends to this day. Connie then began a second career as a psychologist.

Basically, his first marriage ticks all boxes but one. They didn't immediately get married, but all else is textbook. Let's proceed to marriage number two. After his divorce in 1978 and a period of depression, he found love again in 1980, when he met another striking American blonde with a strong English connection (having studied Fine Arts at Oxford); the actress/model Barbara Trentham. She met Cleese when he was performing with *Python* at the Hollywood Bowl.

Surprise, surprise, they hit it off straight away and guess what, she was born in the same year as Connie. Yes, Barbara Trentham was born August 27, 1944, meaning she shared an impressive 10 months of "Partial Confluence". This should mean even more instant attraction than with Connie and the evidence is that they were married after a whirlwind three-month romance in early 1981. All of these life-changing events happened in Barbara's pivotal age 36, "Year of Revolution". Snap again. Cleese marries 24-year-old Connie and then 36-year-old divorcee, Barbara.

This was also a career-defining period for Barbara, as she returned to her second career as a painter and indeed achieved considerable recognition for her work. Yes and to complete the total matrix of correlations, this was the same year that 36-year-old Connie turned her back on comedy, refused to talk about Fawlty, and became seriously involved with mental health, firstly in a film and then later as a student.

I hope I'm not overwhelming you with more and more evidence, but that's how things come at me. It's not drop by patient drop, wrung from hours of dry, academic-style research. It's rather like finding these nuggets of truth simply littering the ground in front of me. To this day, I am simply amazed to have been the first person to uncover this.

We'll now jump ahead to the only instance of a "Window of Opportunity" period for John and Barbara, which happened when he was in his age 48 "Year of Revolution" and she was in her age 43 "Year of Broken Pathways" (i.e., October, 1987 to August, 1988). Could there be a replay of what happened in his first marriage? The *Python Reference Book* tells me that they separated in November, 1987, after arriving in Hollywood to try and sell *A Fish Called Wanda* to a big studio. Barbara went to live just around the corner from John's house in London and they divorced two years later on friendly terms! You should also note in passing, that the release of the *Wanda* movie coincided with Cleese still being in his age 48 "Year of Revolution", making every one of his significant career milestones correlate, viz. *Cambridge Review* hit's the big time at 24, *Fawlty* at 36, and *Wanda* at 48.

These parallels are downright spooky, aren't they? With his marriages, in both cases, there was an effective seven year period till separation. They each had a daughter after a couple of years and both wives pursued new careers. Barbara's settlement was a good deal more generous at 2.5 million pounds, but fell short of what she could have fought for and they remained on good terms. I couldn't find reports of them both being in counselling beforehand, but that doesn't imply that it didn't happen either.

The next question becomes, are we to be three times a charm, or will John's strange life story take a new twist? The essence of "Life Cycles Theory" is that throughout one's life the same themes keep recurring in different forms, with particular reference to standout events every twelve years. Makes you wonder, that life with all its complexities and highways and byways, couldn't possibly be reduced to this one universal formula? That's not what prevailing scientific/rational wisdom tells me, but then again as I've stated before, I'm a bloody-minded independent thinker.

So in 1989, divorce number two is finalised and then in 1990, what do you think happens? Yes, that's right, he's introduced at a party to a vivacious, divorced mother-of-two, Alyce Eichelberger. She's a psychologist who studied at London's Tavistock Institute and another blonde American. They were both addicted to therapy and by that stage, John had even co-written two books with his therapist, Robin Skynner, one being called ironically *Families And How To Survive Them*. Now for the kicker. When do you think Alyce was born? That would be October 28, 1944! Same year as the other two, only this time an unbelievable one day apart! Almost perfect "Partial Confluence" with a 12-month "Window of Opportunity".

Though John was smitten from the get-go, he was understandably a bit more cautious this time around and moved Alyce next door to his place. She was also different from Connie and Barbara, having come from a working class family in Oklahoma, and was then living in a council flat and didn't own a car. She had a mission to climb the social ladder and John was her ready-made answer. They married in December, 1992, when she was in her age 48 "Year of Revolution". This, again, is in a perfect succession. Connie at 24, Barbara at 36, and now Alyce at 48.

Initially, they were a perfect illustration of strong "Partial Confluence". They were both devoted to psychoanalysis, yoga and meditation, and even read the same books together so they could talk about them. Joined at the hip, as the phrase used to go. My question is what might have happened some seven years down the track? They didn't separate so what was it? Also, did Alyce have some form of career change?

It was stated that in 2000, John and Alyce were in marriage counselling, because of issues arising from Cleese's daughter, Camilla, coming to live next door, so there's one box ticked. In addition, Alyce largely abandoned work as a psychologist after her marriage, in favour of social climbing and being called the unit psychologist in *Fierce Creatures*. Most importantly, however, Cleese's 101-year-old mother Muriel, died in this year. He has publicly blamed her cold, domineering personality, for his years of therapy, four marriages and issues with women. All of this happened in John's age 60 "Year of Revolution".

So that was it in a nutshell, now let's bring this up to date. Cleese finally met his match when he separated and then finally divorced Alyce in 2007. She contested the amount and won a staggering 12.5 million pound settlement in 2009, which left her better off than he was and forced him to resume work, performing in an *Alimony Tour* and other things. He never really saw her coming till it was too late.

CONNIE BOOTH
"Partial Confluence"
3 months

BARBARA TRENTHAM
"Partial Confluence"
10 months

DOB: 31.01.1944

DOB: 28.08.1944

JOHN CLEESE

ALYCE EICHELBERGER
"Partial Confluence"
12 months

DOB: 27.10.1939

JENNIFER WADE
"Partial Confluence"
11 ½ months

DOB: 28.10.1944

DOB: 06.10.1980

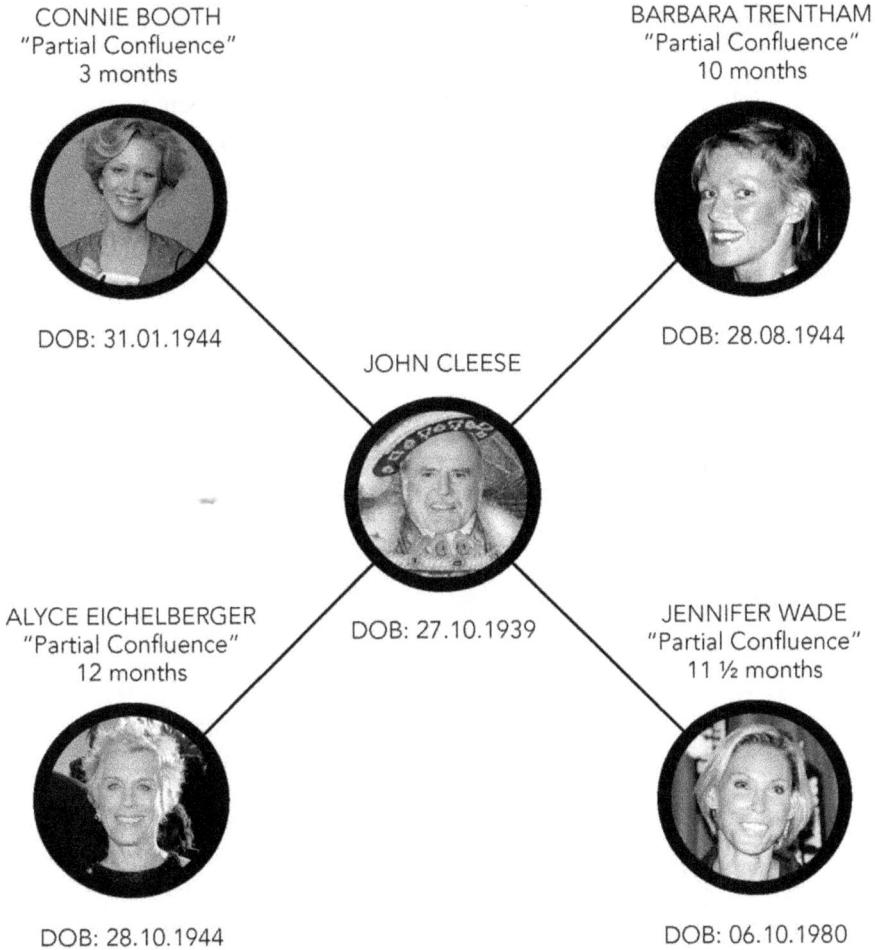

Ever the optimist, however, he found love almost immediately thereafter with, wait for it, another tall, blonde, film and TV actress, American girl, 31 years his junior, Jennifer Wade. The "Life Cycles Theory" punchline is in her date of birth, as it always is. She was born October 6, 1980. Of course, I wouldn't expect you to remember, but what is the answer if you subtract 1944 (year of birth for Connie, Barbara and Alyce) from 1980? It's the magic 36, meaning once again he shared a near perfect 11½ months of "Partial Confluence" with her. They married in August, 2012, when John was in his age 72 "Year of Revolution".

Now that John's angst-ridden childhood has been outed and he is finished with his former soulmate-turned-worst-enemy, the scheming Alyce, the path may finally be cleared for success with his fourth marriage. My only concern would be to check their public records in the years 2019/2020 (i.e., their 7-year mark) to see if there's any trouble. I'm sure you must agree, John is an absolute poster child for "Life Cycles Theory" and he demonstrates the most perfect series of correlations for "Partial Confluence" I have ever seen. Somehow I feel he'd really enjoy all of this analysis if he ever reads it. This concludes our wander through the love lives of some very well-known personalities, and now it's on to show you the true depth of my research.

CHAPTER NINE

STATISTICAL VALIDATION OF LIFE CYCLES

This next chapter is not predominantly related to "Confluence", but it does form the most necessary link in the development of "Life Cycles Theory" as a whole. Since I always stress detailed research to validate my work, I must turn my thoughts to what may be expected by anyone wishing to study my claims.

I can't easily analyse a wide sample of the general population, because there are multiple issues in data collection. I'd need an objective biography of all my subjects, along with quotes by them or about them, to put their lives into proper perspective. It's not quite as simple as asking people did they have a big year when they were 36, or the like, even though I've done this privately and got a lot of positive material. Privacy issues would doubtlessly arise, along with the accuracy of the data.

I really need to be able to substantiate my claims with written biographical records and for that my subjects must possess a number of these. The best way I can study those who are less well-known is to analyse a range of daily obituaries, which is what I have done in Book One. I have also repeated this approach more recently with all obituaries taken over a two week period. It would be too much information to provide you with all their profiles and the chance that you would have heard of any of them is very small.

However, my results have been overwhelmingly positive. So far beyond what statisticians would call the null hypothesis (i.e., that "Life Cycles Theory" doesn't exist), as to be off the scale. For instance, in Book One I analysed 40 obituaries for data on any of the "Significant Years" and achieved a 100% result. Many profiles have multiple years mentioned. I'll show you a brief amount of detail on this.

- Australian author, Glenda Adams, burst upon the literary scene at 36 with her first collection, *Lies And Stories*. At 48, she wins the Miles Franklin Award (Australian equivalent of the Pulitzer Prize).

- The animator, Joseph Barbera, (along with William Hanna the co-creator of Tom and Jerry, The Flintstones, and Yogi Bear). At 36, he bursts upon the scene when *The Cat Concerto* (featuring Tom and Jerry) wins an Academy Award. At 48, *The Flintstones* is released and is their most successful programme.

- Management theorist, Peter Drucker, (known for the 'Peter Principle' in organisations). At 36, he bursts upon the scene when his landmark book, *Concept Of The Corporation*, was published. It was based on a study of the General Motors workforce.

- Colin Fletcher, who was considered the father of the modern backpacking movement. At 36, he treks the length of California, which becomes the basis of his popular first book, *The Thousand Mile Summer*.

- Well-known author, John Fowles, publishes his first breakthrough novel, *The Collector*, at 36.

- Hawaiian entertainer, Don Ho. At 36, he releases his signature hit tune *Tiny Bubbles*.

- Prominent French priest Abbé (i.e., Abbot) Pierre. At 36, he founds the Emmaus organisation, which goes on to operate in 40 countries providing help to poor and homeless people.

- Baron Guy de Rothschild, from the famous family of bankers and businessmen. At 36, he sets about rebuilding the family company after WWII.

- William Russell, inventor of the Russell/Hobbs electric kettle. At 36, he introduces the breakthrough K1 kettle with an elegant modern design. This is one of my favourites.

- Kurt Waldheim, the UN Secretary-General. At 36, he was sent to New York to build a platform for Austria's entry and becomes their first representative, i.e., the birth of his career.

- Jack Wild, British child actor, known for his role as 'The Artful Dodger' in *Oliver*. Prior to 36 he had developed a severe drinking problem that cost him his career, marriage and fortune, along with acquiring diabetes. At 36, he bought a bible and joined Alcoholics Victorious, a God-fearing spin-off of AA (Alcoholics Anonymous). After this, he remained sober and resuscitated his career and life.

- Simon Wiesenthal, the famous Nazi hunter. Although he lived to 96, his whole life is defined by what happened to him at 36. He was a prisoner in the infamous Mauthausen Concentration Camp where 930 of the 1500 inmates died. He felt a profound obligation to those who perished and supplied the American War Crimes Unit with a list of 91 Nazis, including two who behaved decently. He also tracked down his own wife and began his life's work as a Nazi hunter, becoming head of the Jewish Historical Documentation Centre.

I hope you can appreciate the sheer diversity of this short list. A couple of famous names along with others most have never heard of. All, however, share the same life-defining, and career and reputation-making material in their age 36 "Year of Revolution". I have deliberately cherry-picked these examples from the larger list of 40 for their interest value. Many of the others have correlations at 36, as well as numerous other "Significant Years".

In some cases, their obituaries read like a "Life Chart". I found myself listing material relating to ages 12/19/24/31/36/43/48 years and even beyond in some cases. To list all this would conflict with my aim of presenting my group results in an easy-to-understand format. The various likelihoods of say, 6 or more "Significant Years" matching with the short amount of written evidence in one single case is so enormous, I would just about run out of zeros doing the probabilities.

Let me illustrate what I'm talking about with just one obituary from the group of forty. Have any of you heard the name Jean-Jacques Servan-Schreiber? Hardly a household name, unless you are a francophile (lover of all things French) journalist, aged 50 plus. He was a journalist and politician, who founded the prominent French magazine, *L'Express*. In France, he was known simply by his initials JJSS.

A brief obituary of no more than a couple of columns unearthed the following:-

- In his first adult, age 19 "Year of Broken Pathways", he joined Charles de Gaulle's Free French Forces in WWII along with his father, and went to Alabama for training as a fighter pilot. He didn't fly any missions, but he did get his first taste of America and he went on to be a fervent supporter of the American way. This is an easily demonstrable early turning point.

- In his first adult, age 24 "Year of Revolution", he graduated as an engineer, but became fascinated by science and politics, and discovered a taste for writing. He never practised as an engineer. This is the veritable definition of a revolutionary way to acquire your first career identity.

- In his age 31 "Year of Broken Pathways", he was conscripted to Algeria by French President, Pierre Mendès-France, while serving as a shadow councillor. His experiences became the basis of his first book, *Lieutenant En Algérie*. His accounts of brutality were widely circulated and affected the morale of the troops there. He ran these in his newly-founded magazine called *L'Express*.

- In his major midlife, age 36 "Year of Revolution", he travelled to Washington, D.C., several times to meet the newly-elected President John F. Kennedy. He had been one of the first outside of America to write about Kennedy in the '50s, featuring him on the front page of *L'Express*. These meetings were to begin his real life's work, which was to promote American-style trade and business in Europe.

- In his age 43 "Year of Broken Pathways", he published the international best seller, *The American Challenge*, which advocated free trade rather than protectionism and said Europe should copy America.

- In his age 48 "Year of Revolution", he formed a new political alliance of his Radical Party with the Christian Democratic Party, known as the Reforming Movement.

- In his age 55 "Year of Broken Pathways", he quit his own Radical Party to present three candidates for the first European elections under the slogan 'Emploi, Egalite, Europe' (Employment, Equality, Europe). They won only 1.84% of the vote and he decided to retire from politics.

- Finally, in his age 60 "Year of Revolution", he tried to launch a centre for the promotion of information technology, but instead it turned into a money pit and he had to close it down. He moved to Pittsburgh and became associated with the Carnegie Mellon University. This is again, demonstrable revolutionary change in later life, that he was not in control of.

This could fairly be said to represent all the major turning points in his life, as well as showing the likely moments where fate intervened to alter his course. The probability of all this happening by chance is almost beyond comprehension.

Yet all of it was lying in front of me in this short article. No need to conduct in-depth searches, as I sometimes have to. Like finding an intact skeleton of a T-Rex, or the tomb of a Pharaoh, on your first dig.

This is way, way more than merely quoting a life-altering age 36 story. This is real evidence of an intricate, but at the same time very easy to observe, symbolic structure underlying lives. As Einstein himself said, you must be able to state your theory in simple terms.

As a follow up to this data published in 2008, I have subsequently done a much more stringent test on a limited number of defined obituaries. What had concerned me is that in the original sample, I did not include all the obituaries I overviewed. My reasoning was that I wanted to show as much variety in my results as possible. You know, I didn't just want to show a preponderance of authors or actors or politicians.

This does not mean the wider group didn't include some "Significant Year" correlations, it's just that I didn't study them in detail. This time around I wanted to set as tightly controlled a test as I could.

I decided to take just 12 obituaries in sequential order over a two week period, from just one newspaper source. There would be no omissions or add ons. I also wanted to keep just about exclusively to the obituary text for evidence, so there could be every chance that the limited amount of dates mentioned would show no correlations. I'd wager that none of these people you would have heard of, but they had wonderful, fascinating lives nonetheless.

You could say that I had simply 1 chance in 12 (because of my 12-year cycle) with each separate profile to come up with some relevant age 36 data. In reality, it's way less than that because one single important year could happen at almost any adult age, if at all. I decided to use it as a benchmark anyway.

Thus, if "Life Cycles Theory" was simply randomly distributed, I would be happy to come up with one case and very, very lucky if I managed two. The odds for this would be 1 in 12 x 12 = 144.

My results were an astonishing 7 out of 12 cases, which showed verifiable data relating to life and career-defining events in an age 36 "Year of Revolution". I want to stress that this doesn't necessarily mean other cases might not reveal some correlation, but rather that there simply was not enough data to analyse. In one case it wasn't relevant because the individual died at age 34 (he did, however, have a match with age 24 data).

I'm also happy to concede that my formula doesn't fit all people and has to be viewed in the totality of their lives. It's not good enough to be called an exact science. So, if there is a strong match of achievement with an age 24 "Year of Revolution", there shouldn't be a repeat of this at 36, almost by definition. Also, what we do with our lives is always up to us and not all opportunities are realised and, of course, many stand-out events do not happen in the "Significant Years". I do not shirk from examining non-matching data.

So, with that said, let's look at a very basic probability question. If the odds on being very lucky and getting two matches by random chance are 1 in 144, what are these odds like for getting 7 consecutive matches? Using the same method it would be approximately 1 in 35 million. If I only deal with subjects having a public profile that might even cover all, or more than all, of a total population of such profiles. For instance, I'm told the English Wikipedia has around 5 million articles, so 35 million is 7 times this.

Safe to say the odds on this data happening randomly are astronomical. This, however, is only one aspect of "Life Cycles Theory". What I did find is some form of correlation with one or more "Significant Years" in every single profile! If you think I may be exaggerating, because I didn't supply all the details of the study, well there's a reason. It's because that is just the teaser. For the main performance, I want to show the astounding detailed evidence for people you know well, in the form of two objectively derived lists.

The first list is called 'The Ten Most Influential People of the Twentieth Century'. There's a range of these lists and I took one on the basis of its objectivity and appropriateness. I stumbled onto it by accident, because I realised I had been analysing some well-known individuals and I thought, "why not just try and cover all ten subjects, rather than only half?"

Here are my results.

10. Henry Ford.

An automatic inclusion to any list I would have thought. I had already profiled him and came up with positive correlations at every early "Significant Year".

- At 12, his beloved mother dies and he was expected to work on and eventually take over the farm, despite not liking farm work.

- At 19, his direction changes when he becomes adept at operating a Westinghouse portable steam engine and he gets hired by George Westinghouse to service them.

- At 24, he gets married and opens a sawmill, whilst continuing his interest in engineering. This leads him to joining the Edison Illuminating company a few years later.

- At 31, he begins a new direction by devoting his spare time to his personal interest in gasoline engines.

- After several years of trying, he builds one with Edison's support, at the age of 35. What he does next is truly revolutionary. He could have stayed with Edison, some of whose ideas he didn't like, or he could have just continued as an engineer. Instead, at 36, he secured a wealthy backer and founded the Detroit Automobile Company in August, 1899.

- Finally at age 43, after numerous designs didn't prove popular, he embarked on a secret mission to design the ultimate affordable automobile, which of course, became the Model T.

I'm sure you'd agree this evidence is so good, it's almost textbook, but then again it's no better than others like Servan-Schreiber. It works for the simple age 36 statistic and it works for the intricate "Life Chart" compendium.

9. Muhammad Ali Jinnah.

He was an interesting inclusion to the list, but when I learned he was to Pakistan, what Gandhi was to India, I could see their logic. I had never heard of him. I did not do a full analysis, but instead went straight to his age 36 "Year of Revolution" and discovered I really didn't have to go any further. It totally defined his life.

- At 36, he joins the Muslim League and becomes its leader, until the creation of Pakistan. He visits London with Gokhale, the famous Indian statesman, to plead his own case for reform. He becomes known simply as the father of modern day Pakistan.

Another 100% match with "Life Cycles Theory".

8. Mao Zedong.

I personally cannot understand any list not including him. Once again, I knew very little of his life and decided to have a look at his early years.

- In his first adult, age 19 "Year of Broken Pathways", he won a scholarship to the Hunan Teacher's Training College. This was preceded by an unsettled year when he tried and withdrew from a variety of different courses. It was to mark his new direction for the next five years,

- When he was aged 24, he formed the New People's Study Group along with some other revolutionary students, which was a forerunner to the Chinese Communist Party. This could be seen as early evidence of his desire to get involved politically, albeit at a student level. In addition, he graduated and obtained a position as a librarian at Peking University, thanks to his socialist mentor Yang Changji. During this time he also met and fell in love with Yang's daughter Yang Kaihui. All this change and new direction could be equated to the ushering in of his new age.

- His age 36 year (i.e., 1930) was dominated by a local rebellion known as the Futian Incident. This was an important turning point in his career because Soviet-led Chinese Communists were attempting to diminish Mao's peasant-based Communist army. In early December, a Red Army Battalion rebelled against Mao, wrongly claiming he was attempting to surrender to the Nationalists. Their aim was to wipe out his army.

- Mao put down this mutiny with particular savagery, torturing and executing 2,000 to 3,000 dissenters. One month before, in November, Mao's wife, Kaihui, and sister had been captured and beheaded by the Nationalists and he was said to have mourned her for the rest of his life. The origins of Mao's murderous acts throughout his political life could be traced to this and other formative experiences. He learned to strike back hard at his opponents.

Now I grant you this correlation at 36 is not as career and life-defining as many others. It's not like he became leader of the Communist Party after the Long March or similar. I'd be happy to give it half a point, although some may prefer none at all. My early data at 19 and 24, however, correlates well, so this evidence still stands.

7. The Wright Brothers.

As stated in Chapter Six, there is

- ...landmark evidence for older brother, Orville, at 36, with their world-first flight in 1903

- ...and also when Wilbur was 36, with their famous Le Mans flight, which sealed their reputations.

It's a picture perfect correlation.

6. Adolf Hitler.

I have the most intricate and detailed evidence showing linkages of dates (i.e., the "Alignment of the Dates") on the whole life of Hitler at every single adult "Significant Year" (i.e., 19/24/31/36/43/48/55), however I intend to feature him in a future book.

- In summary, at 36, he publishes *Mein Kampf* and dramatically regains control of the Nazi Party in one day (another example of the "One Day Phenomenon"), after almost losing it.

This is a classic example along the lines of Napoleon or Julius Caesar.

5. Winston Churchill.

I have previously written about him.

- At 36, he gets a major promotion as First Lord of the Admiralty. This leads on to the development of tanks, naval aviation, and switching fuel from coal to oil.

4. Franklin D. Roosevelt.

I did a detailed blog article on his age 36 year recently. It was titled simply 'The Day That Almost Changed The Twentieth Century'.

- It showed how his initial decision to divorce Eleanor and marry her secretary Lucy Mercer would have spelt the end of his political career and caused a public scandal. This was only reversed when his domineering mother, Sara, told him he would be disinherited. It was yet another example of the "One Day Phenomenon".

I acknowledge it's a totally different example to most, but it has been the subject of several books and articles, which used the same phrase that I borrowed. My article shows how it totally defined the rest of their personal lives. Franklin (who loved Lucy to the end and died in her arms), Sara, who saw the heavy price it paid on her beloved son; Eleanor, who ceased relations with Franklin, then gathered the strength to challenge Sara and begin her own political career and finally Lucy, who was forbidden to contact Franklin and married someone else, but who was in secret contact with him throughout.

This also shows the subjectivity element of "Life Cycles Theory". Some may prefer to say that his age 36 year didn't correlate with him getting a big promotion or the like, but I would say this amounted to the avoidance of a very large negative in his personal life, that was equally important to his future career. I would score it a full mark but concede that some may give it only a half mark. It is, however, most worthy of a score.

3. Mahatma Gandhi.

He was the subject of intense study, with a detailed "Life Chart", showing every single "Significant Year" in his long life. I also collaborated with an Indian statistician, who studied my results and stated they were significant to the $P = <0.001$ level (i.e., highly significant at the less than one in a thousand level).

- At 36, he organised the first public demonstration of Satyagraha (i.e., non-violent protest) which defined his life. It also became enshrined as the birth of the civil rights movement.

2. Nelson Mandela.

Already featured in Chapter Two. Once again, many of his "Significant Years" have been studied.

- At 36, as you now know, he delivered a famous speech at the Kliptown Conference before several thousand people. He unveiled the Freedom Charter and won his reputation as a statesman.

This totally defined his life.

1. Albert Einstein.

Already featured in *The Life Cycles Revolution* covering every single "Significant Year" in his very famous life.

- At 36, he publishes *Relativity: The Special and the General Theory*, which leads on to the new age of physics and totally defines his life.

So, in this objective list, my coverage is all encompassing. Eight out of ten cases have the most black and white evidence imaginable at 36. Even the other two have partial evidence of big changes at the personal level, which I would concede as half marks in a scientific study.

The odds of this being merely random chance and nothing more, just mount and mount and mount. But even this is not what I want to knock your socks off with. I had been doing blog articles on recent celebrity deaths for some time and decided this would be the perfect foil for a blind study. No Einsteins or Gandhis; more a case of who I heard about on the morning news.

I was at the mercy of whoever died next. I grant you this study is endless, but I'll just take a slice of what I got from the year 2015, until the end of 2016. I have a list of 25 internationally known names. This is a sleeves-rolled-up, pockets-turned-inside-out, study. I'm always happy to examine cases with a lack of evidence. I know I'm not dealing with the laws of physics here and I know I work against the grain. So without further ado, let's proceed.

1. George Martin (died March, 2015)

George was the legendary producer of all *The Beatles* music.

- At 24, he began his career by joining Parlophone Records, working with their classical music division.

- At 31, he began to concentrate exclusively on comedy records.

- At 36, he reluctantly hires *The Beatles* after being petitioned by Brian Epstein. This came to totally define his life and it all happened in one moment of one day, in a textbook example.

- At 43, after seven years of "Unbroken Forward Momentum" *The Beatles* break up, which ends the era.

Every possible box ticked.

2. Leonard Nimoy (died March, 2015)

Previously featured in Chapter Six.

- At 36, *Star Trek* (which totally defined his life) was saved by a fan-driven mail campaign and the rest, as they say, is history.

3. Ben E. King (died April, 2015)

Singer, known for his biggest hit, *Stand By Me*.

- At 24, he leaves Atlantic Records under which he made all his big hits. Begins an era of decline.

- At 36, King (who was reduced to singing in bars and clubs) was accidentally rediscovered by the head of Atlantic, who re-signed him, leading to the comeback hit, *Supernatural Thing*.

- At 48, the movie *Stand By Me* gets released and his hit song gets popular all over again.

A perfect sequence of "Years of Revolution".

4. Christopher Lee (died June, 2015)

Actor, best known for playing Dracula.

- At 24, begins his acting career by default, when it is suggested he join the Rank Organisation.

- At 36, the movie that makes his name, *Dracula*, is released and it leads onto a golden era as a horror actor.

- At 48 and tired of being typecast, he argues with the studio owner and begins doing other movies.

Once again a textbook illustration of "Life Cycles Theory". I have a saying, that at 36 your golden age can be ushered in and then at 48, you effectively leave the stage you have been upon.

5. James Last (died June, 2015)

Last was a German big bandleader and composer.

- At 24, he began his career with Polydor Records as an arranger. He helped arrange hits for many European artists.

- At 36, he released his landmark hit record, *Non-Stop Dancing*, which was a series of brief renditions of popular songs, all tied together with an insistent dance beat. It made him a major European star and he went on to release 190 records, mostly using this genre.

In other words, the pivotal event that defined his whole life, happened again in his age 36 year. I didn't even know about his passing until someone else mentioned his name. Like I said, the gems of "Life Cycles Theory" litter the ground.

6. Omar Sharif (died July, 2015)

He became a major Hollywood star after

- the success of *Lawrence of Arabia*, which this time happened in his age 31 "Year of Broken Pathways". I'm pleased to show this piece of relevant, but non-aligned evidence.

- When he was 36, he created a storm of controversy in the Arab world, when he shared a kiss with Barbra Streisand in *Funny Girl* (it was banned in many Middle Eastern countries).

- As a result, he became estranged from his homeland and lived a glamorous, but largely nomadic, life. In the same year, he tried to make amends by paying for the Egyptian Bridge team (which he captained) to come to France for the World Championships.

7. Cilla Black (died August, 2015)

Most people have heard of this popular singer and TV host.

- At 19, she gets discovered by Brian Epstein (after an initial rejection) and records a string of hit songs.

- At 24, she begins her own TV show, which leads onto a very long and successful second career.

This is a classic case of all her achievement material happening well before her age 36 year.

8. Bart Cummings (died August, 2015)

Legendary Australian racehorse trainer and winner of 12 Melbourne Cups. (The Melbourne Cup is the world's third richest horse race, broadcast in over 160 countries to an estimated 650 million audience.)

- At 36, the horse that made Bart's name, *Light Fingers*, began her amazing run with two Group One victories.

She won the Melbourne Cup in the next year, so this is not a perfect correlation, but it's certainly not out of the ball park either.

9. David Bowie (died January, 2016)

Again Bowie is a household name, whether or not you know much about his music.

- At 24, he began the *Ziggy Stardust* persona, which caught on and catapulted him to fame.

- I'll provide the exact *Wikipedia* quote for his age 36 year (all of the year 1983), "*Bowie reached a new peak of popularity and commercial success in 1983 with the song Let's Dance....the album went platinum in both the UK and US. Let's Dance has sold at least 7 million copies worldwide, making it Bowie's best selling album.*" It turned him into a New Wave icon.

Hard to argue with this example and the more so if you are a Bowie fan.

10. Harper Lee (died February, 2016)

Well-known author of the book, *To Kill a Mockingbird*.

- At 24, she goes to New York, at her childhood friend Truman Capote's urging and commences writing in her spare time.

- At 31, she gets a manuscript called, *Go Set a Watchman*, accepted.

This turns into, *To Kill a Mockingbird*, over the next several years

- ...and at 36, the movie of the book is released, starring Gregory Peck. It becomes a huge success winning an Oscar and being called one of the best films ever made.

Now I grant you, a hard marker may have wanted the book released at 36, but I'm pleased to include an example where there is evidence that is still strong but may be conjectured.

11. Umberto Eco (died February, 2016)

Best-selling author and academic, known for his interest in Semiotics (i.e., the study of signs and symbols).

- At 24, he begins his lecturing career and publishes his first book on St. Thomas Aquinas.

- At 36, he publishes, *The Absent Structure*, which marked his first entry and milestone in the field of Semiotics (i.e, what he is known for).

- At 48, he publishes a runaway best seller, *The Name of the Rose* (again focussing on secret symbols), which gets made into a successful Hollywood movie starring Sean Connery.

He is considered to be the forerunner of Dan Brown. Each new era is perfectly aligned with each successive "Year of Revolution". I was amazed, considering I knew almost nothing of his life beforehand.

12. Prince (died April, 2016)

Not too many people are simply known by one name, but Prince fits the bill.

- At 24, he has a major breakthrough with the album *1999*, which contains some of his biggest hits and catapults him into the musical big league.

- At 36, he begins the split with Warners' Records over not releasing enough of his material. The song, *The Most Beautiful Girl in the World*, commences this and cements his grand passion with the dancer Mayte Garcia. Unfortunately this also commences an era of lessened influence and personal issues, such as the loss of their child, which wrecks his marriage.

This is another case of just about all of the achievement material happening at 24.

13. Reg Grundy (died May, 2016)

A household name in Australia, because of his very successful TV production company. He was an entrepreneur producing and exporting many highly popular game shows (*Sale of the Century*) and soap operas (*Neighbours*). He also began a US production company, selling to NBC.

- At 24, he began his media career as a sports presenter.

- At 36, his production career began, when he pitched his radio game show, *Wheel of Fortune*, to Channel Nine. Since he did not like on-air presenting, he decided to go behind the scenes and founded his own production company, The Reg Grundy Organisation, in the same year. This defined his whole life.

- At 48, he marries his second wife (and grand passion), Joy Chambers.

This represents every key marker of his life again perfectly aligned with his "Years of Revolution".

14. Muhammad Ali (died June, 2016)

Already extensively featured in Chapter Two.

- At 36, he defeats Leon Spinks and becomes the only three-time Heavyweight boxing champion. This follows an ignominious loss to Spinks a few months earlier. He also announces his retirement at the same time.

In terms of how "Years of Revolution" are meant to go, they don't come much better than this.

15. Garry Marshall (died July, 2016)

Principally known as the creator of the mega-popular TV hit show *Happy Days* (and its spin-offs *Laverne and Shirley* and *Mork and Mindy*). He was a writer, producer and director of TV shows and popular movies, such as *Pretty Woman*.

- At 36, he was asked by Paramount to devise a sitcom set in the '20s or '30s. He said he knew nothing of these eras, but suggested the '50s instead. He began writing the pilot of *Happy Days*, which would become what he was known for.

- At 48, *Happy Days* and its spin-offs end (actually *Mork and Mindy* ended in the next year). As a result, he began to concentrate on screenwriting for movies, thus commencing a very successful second era.

This was interesting for me, as I'd never heard of Marshall, but he certainly deserved his mention in the media.

16. Gene Wilder (died August, 2016)

Much loved actor, who was principally known for his breakout role in the ever-popular, *Willy Wonka and the Chocolate Factory*.

- At 36, Wilder was the last in a long line of big name actors who were considered, but rejected, for the lead role of Willy. He was not a star then and had only one poorly received movie to his name.

- Welcome to the one day that would change his life forever (i.e., the

"One Day Phenomenon"). Director Mel Stuart and producer David L. Wolper had an agreement that no offers would be made at auditions. However, as soon as Wilder walked into the room, Stuart knew he was the one. When he did a reading it only convinced him further.

- Stuart forgot about their arrangement and chased Wilder down the corridor, reaching him just before he got into the lift. He said, "You're doing this picture, no two ways about it. You're Willy Wonka!"

I just love this story. It exemplifies the element of fate and not being fully in control of events in a "Year of Revolution" better than anything else I know.

17. Fidel Castro (died November, 2016)

So well-known he needs no introduction.

- At 36, he became embroiled in the Cuban Missile Crisis, when he secretly let Russia install nuclear missiles as a way of ensuring safety and enhancing the socialist cause. When US aerial reconnaissance picked it up, it led to a full-blown international crisis.

- The US then did a deal with Russia, that saw the missiles withdrawn in exchange for not invading Cuba. Castro was received as a hero in Moscow, being awarded the Order of Lenin. He brought back many new ideas and it began a very productive new era as President.

They don't come much more high profile and earth-shattering than this example.

18. Florence Henderson (died November, 2016)

Known for her role as mum in *The Brady Bunch*, a hit TV show. Now this is a classic case of close but no cigar, since *The Brady Bunch* began airing 5 months before Florence turned 36. Since this is what she was known for, on the surface, this one is clearly a miss. I am left with a more erudite question, "did anything of significance happen in her age 36 year?"

- When I did the analysis, it turned out that the movie, *Song of Norway*, starring Florence, was released in 1970 (her age 36 birthday was on February 14). This was a film adaptation of an operetta based on the life of Edvard Grieg. At the time she was a major Broadway star and an acclaimed soprano, and they tried to turn it into *Sound of Music* 2.

- In spite of an international cast, it was a monumental flop, with one critic saying, "this movie is of an unbelievable badness, it brings back cliches you didn't know you knew..." Suffice it to say, Florence's movie career was nipped in the bud. Meanwhile, it was on her parallel track, with this then-fledgling TV sitcom, that her future fame lay.

- You wouldn't have known this in 1970 though, since *The Brady Bunch* original run got mostly negative reviews and never made the Nielsen top 30. So back in those days, everything was in the balance for Florence. She wanted to be a star of a hit musical like *Sound of Music*, but instead was stuck with this below average TV show.

This is a great illustration of my principle of doing a full analysis and not just relying on a summary overview which produces a negative result. You can score this one as you please, but I'd say 1970 was a pretty pivotal year in Florence's life.

19. Leonard Cohen (died November, 2016)

Leonard was a singer, songwriter, poet and novelist, who was known for his sombre and intense material.

- At 36, he released his third album *Songs of Love and Hate*, which received great reviews and was his most commercially successful record. It performed well in many parts of the world, reaching No. 4 in the UK and No. 8 in Australia. It also sealed his reputation for emotional intensity.

- Also at 36, the highly acclaimed Robert Altman movie *McCabe and Mrs. Miller* was released featuring three Leonard Cohen songs, which were said to "unify the entire movie." Again they were mournful ballads, further cementing his reputation.

No question, all this material was a high watermark of Leonard's career.

20. George Michael (died December, 2016)

Michael was a popular and successful singer and songwriter, who was widely known.

- At 24, he released his first solo smash hit album *Faith*, following a successful career with the duo, *Wham*. It topped the UK Albums chart and had 12 weeks as number one on the US Billboard 200. He had truly come of age as an international solo star in this year. Rather like what Prince did at the same age.

- At 36, there was a distinct turnabout in his fortunes, again similar to Prince. He released his last album through Virgin Records, *Songs From The Last Century*. It performed very poorly at 157 on the American Billboard chart and led onto a hiatus of a couple of years in his recording career.

- Also, there was continuing fallout from his conviction for lewd behaviour in a Los Angeles toilet the year before. As a result of releasing a single called *Outside*, which mocked the arresting officer, the officer brought a $10 million lawsuit against the singer. Again this was eventually dismissed after a couple years.

This is yet another case of a lot of the achievement material happening at 24, which is then followed by a turnabout in fortunes at 36. It's not always guaranteed, of course, and depends on a mix of all the elements of the person's life.

21. John Glenn (died December, 2016)

Famous astronaut and United States Senator. He was the first American to orbit the earth in 1962, circling it three times.

This is going to be another case of looking more closely at the detail, because Glenn was well past 36 (i.e., the period July, 1957 to July, 1958) when he orbited the earth. So, similarly to Florence Henderson, we will ask the question, "what, if anything, happened when he was 36?"

I'm going to quote now from an obituary in an official blog called *Spaceflight Insider*.

- *"Glenn first came to the attention of the public, when he conducted the first supersonic transcontinental flight in July, 1958...The flight took some 3 hours, 23 minutes and 8.3 seconds - and made Glenn a celebrity."*

It would lead onto Glenn being selected as one of the original 'Mercury Seven' astronauts in the next year. Once again, you can score this as you will, but it is certainly a breakout moment in Glenn's budding career as an astronaut.

22. Henry Heimlich (died December, 2016)

Heimlich was an American thoracic surgeon and medical researcher. He is widely credited as the pioneer of the emergency medical procedure for stopping choking, known as the Heimlich Maneuver. He was also a controversial figure, who courted publicity and operated largely outside the medical establishment. I really have uncovered the wild and wacky world of Henry Heimlich, but there simply isn't space to include it.

One year before he turned 36 (i.e., most of the year 1955), he proposed a method of restoring a patient's lost ability to swallow, by using a section of the patient's stomach. His article in the *American Journal of Surgery* was virtually ignored, but a Romanian surgeon wrote, saying he had been using this procedure for four years.

- In his age 36 year, he was invited by the Romanian Academy of Sciences to review the procedure. He returned to New York, successfully tried the operation and it became a standard procedure in America.

- This was his best-ever reception by the medical establishment, who queried his Heimlich Maneuver for many years, along with other unusual offshoots, such as using malariotherapy to treat cancer.

23. Zsa Zsa Gabor (died December, 2016)

She was famous for being famous, as the phrase goes. The forerunner of a string of similar media personalities in the current age, but distinctive for her witty and engaging style. She was a one of a kind star. However, my analysis reveals she almost did consolidate herself as a Hollywood actress, until her personal life brought it all undone.

- Welcome to the year 1953, when for most of it Zsa Zsa was 36. In this year she had the last of her small number of serious film credits with the musical *Lili*, which was MGM's most successful film of the year. She had begun her acting career through her third husband George Sanders, who was a well-known character actor. He introduced her to his agent in Hollywood, who could see some potential in her wit and style.

- Her personal life was always going to get in the way, however. Sanders was a noted philanderer (his autobiography was called *Memoirs of a Professional Cad*), but he was also the husband Zsa Zsa was said to have loved the most. As a couple before marriage, they became firm friends with the Dominican diplomat and playboy, Porfirio Rubirosa, and his wife at the time, Doris Duke.

- Sanders had a romance with Doris, which Zsa Zsa eventually found out about. As a result, in the year before, 1952, she announced she was going to have an affair with Porfirio, who was by now divorced. This became an unseemly mess when Zsa Zsa, while still married to Sanders, demanded Porfirio marry her. They fought and as a result, there is a photo of her with a black eye, taken at a press conference the next day.

- Instead, Porfirio married the Woolworth's heiress Barbara Hutton in late 1953 and it lasted only 55 days. It was reported that he and Zsa Zsa were still carrying on, even on the night of the honeymoon. Suffice it to say, she was dropped by her agent and relegated to a range of fringe films and projects thereafter.

If you like all this stuff, then don't worry I'll have Zsa Zsa back at the after party.

24. Carrie Fisher (died December, 2016)

Already featured in Chapter Six.

- At 19, she is discovered in the movie *Star Wars*.

- At 24, she reaches her height of fame, with the second Star Wars' smash hit *The Empire Strikes Back*.

- At 36, she gives birth to her daughter, Billie Lourd, discovers her husband is gay and not long after he leaves her for a man.

25. Debbie Reynolds (died December, 2016)

Also featured in Chapter Six.

- At 19, she gets discovered with a Golden Globe for Most Promising Actress in *Three Little Words*, as well as having a hit record with the song *Aba Daba Honeymoon*.

- At 24, she gives birth to daughter Carrie and cracks are beginning to appear in her recent marriage to Eddie Fisher.

- At 36, she attempts unsuccessfully to begin a TV series called *The Debbie Reynolds Show*, made in the style of *I Love Lucy*.

- This gets repeated at 60, with the unsuccessful launch of The Debbie Reynolds Hotel in Las Vegas.

This ends my extensive list, with a surge in entries for the last month of December, 2016. I'm not going to attempt probabilities, because it is up to you to judge for yourself if this constitutes overwhelming evidence of the reality of "Life Cycles Theory". I have presented case after case after case, with either definitive evidence, or certainly very relevant supporting evidence. There is not one single exception. None! Think about the implications of this.

I have shown you black and white evidence of life and career-defining material at age 36, for George Martin, Leonard Nimoy, Christopher Lee, James Last, David Bowie, Umberto Eco, Reg Grundy, Muhammad Ali, Garry Marshall, Gene Wilder, Fidel Castro and Leonard Cohen. That's 12 out of 25 cases or around 50% of the sample. If I only used this one feature of "Life Cycles Theory" random chance would say I shouldn't even find one case.

In addition, I have shown you a career high watermark and commencement of reputation at 24 and sometimes at 19, for Cilla Black, Prince, George Michael, Carrie Fisher, and Debbie Reynolds. That takes us up to 17 out of 25 cases with black and white evidence. That's about two-thirds of our sample. Next, I have shown you strong but conjectural evidence at 36, for Ben E. King, Bart Cummings, Harper Lee, Florence Henderson, John Glenn, Henry Heimlich, Zsa Zsa Gabor and to a lesser extent Omar Sharif. This brings the total to 25 and is therefore 100% coverage! It also doesn't include the many related "Significant Years" that were mentioned.

There are 49 examples above of relevant data confirming most aspects of "Life Cycles Theory" for only 24 cases. You can see how in some instances every minute detail of the theory is covered. This is a motherlode of evidence in a totally random group. Once again, just let that settle in for a moment.

Now we are going to compare and contrast my detailed and extensive data with the only other material to acquire a noted public profile in the area of unseen influences in our lives and destinies. How many of you remember newspaper reports and even a TV documentary on the so-called 'Mars Effect'?

This was the life's work of a French psychologist and academic by the name of Michel Gauquelin. Because he was an academic insider, with influential friends like the well-known psychologist Hans Eysenck, numerous papers and presentations occurred. He challenged the sceptics establishment, who devoted years and years of effort to disprove what he was advocating.

This was all in the name of the totally discredited occult system of astrology. Gauquelin, who didn't even believe in most of astrology, said he had proof that one aspect of it was true. Astrologers saw it as the thin end of the wedge. If one bit could be proven true, then the rest could be as well by inference.

This was a purported statistical correlation, between athletic eminence and the position of the planet Mars on the horizon, at the time and place of birth. Gauquelin identified two sectors out of twelve, where he saw a somewhat larger number of births of champion athletes. Later studies were inconclusive because attempts to replicate it produced uneven results, along with problems concerning the criterion of eminence.

However, while all this was alive and kicking, good old astrology began to see other possible relationships. If Mars, which was somehow mysteriously to do with war, bred athletes; then maybe Saturn, which was said to be a serious and stern planet (all made up of course), might have a preponderance of eminent scientists. Why stop there, I mean the beautiful Venus, could have a larger number of eminent artists and communicative Mercury could have a bunch of writers.

It all got very out of hand. The problem with the sceptics is they showed their easily offended underbelly. There was never any need to conduct extensive validation studies, because there was no rational or scientific proof that astronomical bodies can influence our behaviour. It's as simple as that. Even if there were some correlations shown, then it would come down to the maxim, that correlation does not prove causation. End of story.

Check it out for yourselves and you will see that from 1956 until 1996 (that is an unbelievable 40 years), various studies at first seemed to support and then dismissed Gauquelin's work. What interests me is not this whole period. What interests me, is what exactly did they call statistical significance in the first place? In 1977, from a random group of 100 athletes (chosen from a group of around 2,000), a Professor Zelen found that the Mars-in-the-key-sector's expectation was 17% for the total population, but was 22% in the sample.

Yes, 17% is simply a one in six random chance and he was making a big deal over it being a mere 5% more than this! How statistically significant was this? Well, it's not $P => 0.001$ (that my data on Gandhi's life showed) and it's not $P => 0.01$ that's for sure. It's not even $P => 0.1$.

More like just one-third higher than you might imagine. It would be akin to me saying, I have shown 1.33 cases of the "Age 36 Phenomenon" in all of my sample groups. This is a ridiculously small result to get publicised. If this was the best I could do, I'd give up in embarrassment. In short, you don't need a degree in math to see it's not a big deal. For this, it got 40 years of statistical reviews, world news coverage and a TV documentary?!

Funny isn't it? I've asked several sceptics programmes and academics to have a look at my results without any reply. The most recent was just as I was reviewing this passage; when I challenged an article on coincidences and the concept called 'synchronicity' (i.e., deriving meaning from subjective linkages of otherwise random events).

We can do this as an idle exercise at any time, when we say things like, "what a coincidence". An example would be someone else mentioning a person you were just thinking of, or the same number sequence that keeps showing up. We sometimes supply our own meaning after the event by suggesting, "there must be some meaning to this". Statisticians tell us that with 7 billion people in the world, many strange and wacky events are going to happen every day, but it is perfectly normal and doesn't signify anything.

This is the exact opposite of "Life Cycles Theory", which studies verifiable biographical data about life-defining events against a predetermined framework without the person having to participate. I only need a well-documented record and maybe a direct quote.

I showed the author of the article on coincidences my detailed rebuttal, by using the life of well-known psychologist Carl Jung (the originator of the term 'synchronicity'), which happened to be yet another landmark case of the "Age 36 Phenomenon", this time for his own life.

When he was 36, he argued with his mentor Freud and published his most important work *The Psychology of the Unconscious*, which marked the birth of his own theory, known as 'Analytical Psychology'. That's "Life Cycles Theory" in action and it's not a mere coincidence, or the totally subjective notion called 'synchronicity'. It's a hard biographical fact, which is dramatically shown in the movie, *A Dangerous Method*.

Not a peep out of them, when I offered them an opportunity to critique my work, which of course I'm quite used to. I've even had my books reviewed by the two universities that I attended, with good feedback and no negative comments. I want you to be your own open-minded judges. You'll know the truth of my theory because you will simply be overwhelmed by its widespread evidence. Your conclusion would be based on your own common sense.

Would it make any difference to you if I was more well known? I hope the answer is no, as I consider it's even better this way. You see my relative ordinariness is what should impress you more. As a footnote to this chapter, I will give you a story from my early days as a second-year student of psychology.

I had decided early on, that I wanted a career as a psychologist, and set about doing as well as I could in the annual exams. In fact, I was told that I had just missed out on a chance to do honours, as I was the first to miss the cut-off. I was allowed to appeal to the Dean of Arts, which I did, but the decision stood.

If I had done honours and then a doctorate, I might have joined the ranks of Gauquelin and got lots of academic exposure for my writings. But on the other hand, I'd never have worked in the real world and "Life Cycles Theory" was derived from my work in my own outplacement company. In retrospect, it simply wasn't my path and I'm glad it turned out this way.

I felt a certain affinity with Michel Gauquelin, as I too was mesmerised by astrology in the '70s and '80s and had many books on the subject. He was also a very talented tennis player, a sport I have played competitively and socially my whole life.

I was sad to read that he had a nervous breakdown in 1991 at the age of 61 (following the 1990 Committee for the Study of Paranormal Behaviour leaked report, confirming no 'Mars effect'). He had ordered all his files destroyed and then committed suicide. This is such a waste of a fine life, but also an object lesson to others, to make their case for any unseen influences on lives in a truly comprehensive manner.

The bottom line is, once again, I don't know what, if anything, causes my strange set of correlations and quite frankly I don't much care. "Life Cycles Theory" is scientifically-based but not as exact, as say, physics. It is in no way a mere occult system. I can't simply be dismissed by the 'correlation does not prove cause' phrase, since I don't deal in causes. I only deal in correlations and as you can see, with me it's correlations by the bucketful.

CHAPTER TEN

SUMMARY AND CONCLUSION

We're going to revisit all the terms used so far and reinforce their meanings for you. I do this because my theory consists of totally new jargon. It's easy to understand, but nothing beats repeating the message. I'm always careful to use language that says what it means. Statisticians would call this good face validity.

So let's list them out. I simply use inverted commas for emphasis, as I did throughout the text.

1. "Life Cycles Theory"- the whole body of terms, explanations and supporting evidence of the theory.

2. "One Day Phenomenon"- evidence that the "Moment of Breakthrough/Achievement" in a "Year of Revolution" happens in one day.

3. "Alignment of the Dates"- evidence that important changes taking place in "Significant Years" tend to occur around the same time in each separate twelve-year cycle.

4. "Age 36 Phenomenon"- evidence that changes in an age 36 "Year of Revolution" are so profound, that they come to define a person's whole life.

5. "Year of Revolution"- the first year in each twelve-year cycle. It equates to the ages of 12,24,36,48, etc., and represents the ushering in of a new age/direction.

6. "Moment of Setback/Frustration"- this usually occurs first in a "Year of Revolution". It is a low point and represents the symbolic death of the old cycle.

7. "Moment of Breakthrough/Achievement"- this follows the low point, usually in one day and is accompanied by feelings of euphoria.

8. "Year of Broken Pathways"- this occurs seven years after the "Year of

Revolution" and brings about direction change and challenge in a gradual manner. It equates to ages 7,19,31,43, etc.

9. "Unbroken Forward Momentum"- refers to the seven-year period between a "Year of Revolution" and a "Year of Broken Pathways".

10. "Subjective Evidence"- a quote from the person whose life is being analysed i.e., from the subject.

11. "Objective Evidence"- any reputable biographic information from a variety of sources.

12. "Life Chart"- a graphical representation of collated "Years of Revolution" and "Years of Broken Pathways" along with their common themes.

13. "Significant Years"- all "Years of Revolution" and "Years of Broken Pathways" i.e., 7/12/19/24/31, etc.

14. "Substantive Similarity"- straightforward similarity between events in successive "Years of Revolution" and separately for "Years of Broken Pathways".

15. "Symbolic Similarity"- less obvious similarity, looking for common underlying themes in successive "Years of Revolution" and separately for "Years of Broken Pathways".

16. "Confluence"- an overlap of the "Significant Years" shared by two or more people, who are in some form of relationship. It should promote greater empathy and understanding.

17. "Full Confluence"- an overlap of the "Years of Revolution" between two or more people, e.g., they could be born within twelve months of each other, or any multiple of twelve (i.e., 12/24/36, etc.) years apart. They would be "Confluent" for every shared "Significant Year".

18. "Partial Confluence"- an overlap between two or more people for any "Year of Revolution" and "Year of Broken Pathways". They would only be "Confluent" for every second shared "Significant Year".

19. "Window of Opportunity"- the period of months shared by two people when they are "Confluent". During this time things can go one way or another.

20. "Real Time"- to be aware of events in your "Significant Years" as they occur.

21. "Real Time Confluence"- to be aware of events between you and someone you are "Confluent" with, as it occurs.

22. "Fated Relationship"- to meet your life partner during a period of "Confluence".

23. "Whorl of Confluence"- three or more people who have shared periods of "Confluence".

In addition to displaying my statistical results in the previous chapter, I am now going to briefly summarise my results for this book. Primarily I have featured an array of famous couples, family pairings, friendships and career-related cases, where some form of "Confluence" was present. I even included a small number of worst enemy, rather than best friend, examples.

The aim is to show how "Confluence" can impact every area of our lives and not just how to help people find their ideal romantic partner. In fact, I go to great lengths to say that only a small number of successful unions are marked by "Confluence". Like everything else with "Life Cycles Theory", you simply can't make it happen.

I hate to disappoint those who want a quick fix for just about all of life's dramas, but if you are fortunate enough to see that a certain person you really like is "Confluent" with you, then this could become a "Fated Relationship".

Even the most "Confluent" of couples can still break up and in many cases remain good friends, because the shared empathy, resulting from facing your upheavals and challenges together, will not change. Even worst enemies can end up with a degree of mutual respect and admiration.

The real magic of this book is the sheer number of highly improbable results I have obtained, simply by analysing some of history's greatest romances, both ancient and modern. I would not even have had enough subject matter to fill a book if I hadn't been able to produce some amazing evidence of "Confluence" throughout the ages. As I am also at pains to point out, some of what I write about is well planned and researched, sometimes years beforehand; but other examples I just do on the run as I am writing. A very good case was Victoria and Albert. The best way I can convey my own exuberance at these accidental discoveries is to say so at the time.

So here is a summary of my famous couples, and families and friends, that are all on the public record and easily verifiable.

1. Prince William and Catherine, the Duke and Duchess of Cambridge. The poster couple of "Confluence".

- They met in a "Window of Opportunity" at 19,

- ...briefly broke up and reunited around their shared age 24 "Years of Revolution"

- ...and faced their own challenges and direction changes in their shared age 31 "Years of Broken Pathways".

If you said to me, "so what is a good example of this theory?" I'd simply point to this famous couple and say, "it's them."

2. John F. Kennedy (JFK) and Jackie.

Surely one of the twentieth century's great love stories, even if marred by many infidelities.

- They met in a "Window of Opportunity" at 31/19,

- ...were married and faced JFK's serious back surgeries at 36/24

- ...and shared the challenges of the closely fought 1960 presidential election and its aftermath together at 43/31.

3. Humphrey Bogart and Lauren Bacall.

A couple synonymous with love song lyrics, they were an incredibly unlikely long term match. They also

- ...met in a "Window of Opportunity" in their respective "Years of Broken Pathways" at 19 and 43.

Like William and Catherine, and JFK and Jackie, they all would qualify as a "Fated Relationship".

4. Charlie Chaplin and Oona O'Neill.

Not as well-known, but this is the most unbelievable love story of all.

- They had a rare 36-year age difference and notwithstanding Chaplin's notorious reputation with young actresses, they completely fell in love for the rest of their shared lives on the spot. They also shared the greatest amount of "Confluence" of all couples and were each other's best friends.

5. Liz Taylor and Richard Burton.

They shared three months of "Partial Confluence" and met when Burton was in his age 36 year. Their tempestuous relationship made many headlines,

- ...but they only shared one small period of "Confluence", that featured a family drama and health issues for Burton, and what amounted to the end of her golden era for Liz.

A very good example of it being better to have more "Confluence" than less.

6. Spencer Tracy and Katharine Hepburn.

They shared a strong 11 months of "Partial Confluence" and remained a committed couple, if in the form of an open, but nominally secret, relationship.

- They were each other's best friends and defenders till Spencer's death.

- Tracy was also "Confluent" with best friend Bogart, and both couples were "Confluent" as well, making it a truly agreeable foursome.

7. Victoria and Albert.

The subject of many books, films and TV specials, this was truly a royal match for the ages. So close were they, that they virtually ruled as a joint couple. They were amazingly "Confluent".

- At their combined age 24 "Years of Revolution", they faced a diplomatic crisis over French treatment of a British Consul.

- At their combined age 31 "Years of Revolution", they opened the famous Great Exhibition of Science and Industry, as an initiative of Albert's.

- At their combined age 36 "Years of Revolution", they overcame criticism about marriage of their daughter to a Prussian Prince by initiating the Victoria Cross.

8. Juan and Eva Peron.

One of recent history's most famous, if tragic, couples. They had a 24-year age gap and were "Confluent" for seven out of twelve months.

- They met in a "Window of Opportunity" when Juan was 48 and Eva was 24.

No doubt about it, they were a "Fated Relationship" if ever there was one.

9. Joe DiMaggio and Marilyn Monroe.

An unlikely couple because of their short and disastrous marriage. However, they remained friends and supporters until the end of both their lives, and there is very strong evidence that they were on the verge of getting re-married, just days before Marilyn's death.

- Joe is the only person, who Marilyn was married to or had a longer term relationship with, that she shared any "Confluence" with.

- Tragically, they never saw such a period of "Confluence", that would have come only months after her death.

10. Marc Antony and Cleopatra.

Though they did not share any "Confluence", they were both, in fact, "Confluent" with Julius Caesar.

- When Caesar was in his age 55 "Year of Broken Pathways" and Cleopatra was in her age 24 "Year of Revolution", they were on the verge of marriage and Caesar becoming Emperor, which was just before he was murdered. You can see it all in the movie.

- When Cleopatra was 36, she tried to establish an independent power base with Marc Antony, leading to a Senate inquiry, which declared war on them.

11. Henry VIII and Anne Boleyn.

They didn't share any "Confluence" either. The only one of Henry's wives to be "Confluent" with him was Catherine of Aragon.

- There is evidence that Henry and Catherine had a good relationship for many years, until Catherine regrettably hired Anne Boleyn to Henry's Court in her age 36 "Year of Revolution" and Henry's age 31 "Year of Broken Pathways".

12. George Clooney and Amal Alamuddin.

They share nine months of "Partial Confluence".

- Their whirlwind engagement and marriage took place in Amal's age 36 "Year of Revolution".

13. Armstrong, Aldrin and Collins.

All three famous astronauts for the history making 1969 Moon landing were born in the same year

- ...and were a poster example of a "Confluent" work team, as this difficult journey relied on great teamwork.

14. Abraham Lincoln and John J. Hardin.

Both these aspiring politicians were in their combined age 36 "Years of Revolution" together for only one month,

- ...but this is the critical period when the election of a Whig nomination for Washington was determined. It really began Lincoln's national career.

15. *The Seinfeld Show.*

All four main cast members were "Confluent" with each other, making for a truly harmonious working environment, as the show itself depicts.

- The show was properly launched in a period of "Confluence" and also ended in one.

16. James Watson and Francis Crick.

Pioneering scientists, who discovered the composition of the genetic code. They had "Full Confluence" for almost 11 out of 12 months.

- The discovery of their double helix model was made during a "Window of Opportunity", when Crick was 36 and Watson was 24.

17. Larry Page and Sergey Brin.

Founders of Google. They were born in the same year and shared seven months of "Full Confluence".

- At 24, they created the Google name by accident and tried unsuccessfully to sell it to Yahoo.

- At 31, they both became very wealthy with the company going public.

- At 36, they had different personal achievements that reflected their priorities. This was the period when Page had won back his reputation with the Android phone, leading onto resuming as CEO.

18. Sergey Brin and Anne Wojcicki.

Formerly married, these two share an amazing 11 months of "Full Confluence" (like Chaplin and O'Neill). They were initially called 'the twins', they were so alike, which is a perfect description of the friendship and romance sides of "Confluence" combined.

- At 31, they founded the Brin-Wojcicki Foundation committed to finding a cure for Parkinson's Disease after Brin's mother became afflicted.

- At 36, they combined the Foundation with Anne's DNA testing company, 23andMe, to provide the largest Parkinson's research study.

After divorce, they are still good friends and live close by, again showing this residual side of "Confluence".

19. J.K. Rowling and Kevin Tsujihara.

They were "Confluent" for only three months in 2013 (when they were both aged 48) ,

- ...but this is when Kevin, the newly appointed CEO of Warner's, did a deal with Rowling for the movie franchise built on her short book called *Fantastic Beasts And Where To Find Them*. Rowling was allowed to write the screenplay, which was a first.

- The success of the first movie now has at least four sequels planned. Nobody believed that Kevin, who came from the distribution side of the business, could do this deal.

20. Wilbur and Orville Wright.

A standout example of "Confluence" in families.

- The first powered, heavier-than-air flight happened when Wilbur was in his age 36 year

- ...and they perfected their lightweight engine in a "Window of Opportunity" period when Orville was 31.

- Their famous Le Mans flight, which sealed their reputations, happened in Orville's age 36 year.

21. Charles and Louis Comfort Tiffany.

This amazing father and son were almost totally "Confluent", being born three days apart.

- At 24/48, Louis launched his art career with his father's backing, even though Charles wanted him to take over his business.

- At 36/60, Louis closed his interior design company and took steps to open his famous glass company, once again with his father's backing.

This example of "Confluence" in families is near perfection.

22. Floyd May weather Senior and Junior.

This famous father and son boxing dynasty, showed a remarkable path of

- ...joining together at 12/36,

- ...splitting up for many years at 24/48

- ...and then reuniting when they were 36/60.

Every date and every family drama fits the "Confluence" model to a tee.

23. William Shatner and Leonard Nimoy.

This pair of bosom buddies were born within four days of each other.

- They both went through the low point of the newly-launched *Star Trek* being cancelled and then miraculously saved by a fan-driven mail campaign, during their joint age 36 years.

- They remained the closest of friends till Leonard's recent death.

24. Carrie Fisher, Debbie Reynolds, and Billie Lourd.

The three generations of this well-known showbiz family were all "Confluent".

- The recent deaths of Carrie and Debbie, happened when they were 60 and 84 respectively and Billy was aged 24.

- Billy was born just prior to Carrie's age 36 year, which coincided with the breakdown of her marriage to a husband who was gay.

- At the same time a 60-year-old Debbie was embarking on an ill-fated venture, buying a Las Vegas hotel.

25. Debbie Reynolds and Liz Taylor.

This was a very unlikely instance of lifelong friendship between two amazingly "Confluent" people, born two days apart.

- Debbie was the injured party when Liz stole her then-husband, Eddie Fisher. However, they made up in 1966 and remained close friends till Liz's death.

- Liz, who always felt some guilt over Fisher, left Debbie some valuable jewelry in her estate.

26. Hannibal Barca and Scipio Africanus.

They had almost identical upbringings and with some allowance for inexact dates of birth, were most probably "Confluent" in some history-making episodes of the Second Punic Wars.

- At 31/19, they took part in the bloody battle of Cannae on opposite sides. Hannibal destroyed Rome's army and only young Scipio's daring tactics saved a total surrender.

- At 36/24, Hannibal failed in his only siege of Rome, while Scipio was promoted to general and proconsul to avenge his father's death in Spain at the hands of Hannibal's brother.

- At 43/31, Scipio became a full consul and persuaded the Senate to let him invade Carthage. This caused Hannibal to be recalled and led to their final showdown.

27. Arthur Wellesley and Napoleon Bonaparte.

These two were born three months apart in the same year. This means they were very "Confluent". Their paths did not really cross until Lieutenant-General Wellesley became commander of a force of 9,000 men in Spain during the Peninsula War.

- When he was 43, he decisively beat Napoleon's brother, Joseph, who was then the King of Spain, coinciding with the disastrous Russian campaign. Arthur was promoted to Field Marshall and became the Duke of Wellington,

- ...while Napoleon stated his woes in Europe could be tied to this defeat, done by his ultimate conqueror.

- Each man also had a year of intrigue, that could have changed the fates of both of them at 48.

28. Brad Pitt, Jennifer Aniston, Angelina Jolie, and Marion Cotillard.

All of these famous actors were "Confluent" with different "Windows of Opportunity" coinciding with the direction of their personal lives.

- Brad married Jen when he was 36 and she was 31, and they were considered Hollywood's golden couple.

- When Jen was 36, her world came crashing down when Pitt became involved with Jolie and they quickly divorced.

- When Pitt was 48 and Jolie was 36, they announced their intention to get married.

- At the same time Aniston, who was 43, became engaged to Justin Theroux.

- Pitt and Jolie's pending divorce happened at a time when Pitt was suspected of a possible relationship with his co-star, Marion Cotillard. Pitt and Cotillard were even more "Confluent" than he was with Jolie. Even though nothing came of this, it was an unsettling period.

29. Tom Cruise, Mimi Rogers, Nicole Kidman, and Katie Holmes.

All three of Tom's marriages feature the same "Partial Confluence", although it is strongest with Nicole. All three marriages also feature the same conflicts with Tom's Scientology beliefs. There is a marked similarity between each case.

Each "Window of Opportunity" features,

- Tom being introduced to the religion through Mimi at 24,

- ...being forcibly drawn away from Nicole because of the religion at 36,

- ...and Katie expressing her independence from the religion when Tom was 48.

30. John Cleese, Connie Booth, Barbara Trentham, Alyce Eichelberger, and Jennifer Wade.

John shared the same "Partial Confluence" with all four of his wives. In fact, the first three were all born in the same year, share mostly similar backgrounds and interests, as well as physical appearance. His story is so bizarre it could only come from real life.

- His "Windows of Opportunity" tend to coincide with the breakdown of his relationships, hopefully with the exception of his current marriage.

- Each of his first three wives got married in successive "Years of Revolution"; Connie at 24, Barbara at 36, and Alyce at 48.

Following this shortened version of the many well-known relationships that were analysed, I will mention the many instances of relevant "Significant Years" for various subjects, which are littered throughout the text. These constitute very valuable evidence and will be listed separately for you.

In many cases, the analysis was done as I wrote about them and I was as surprised as anyone with what I found. I have effectively produced an almost encyclopaedic coverage of my subjects, which I would happily hand to any independent investigator. It should only serve to make most readers pay even more attention to my final contentious remarks.

1. Napoleon Bonaparte.

- At 24, he wins the Siege of Toulon and is promoted from Major to Brigadier General.

- At 36, he wins his greatest-ever victory at Austerlitz in one day and gains control of Europe.

2. Joy Mangano.

- TV marketing guru and subject of the movie *Joy*. At 36, her whole life was turned around in a single day, all of which conforms exactly with "Life Cycles Theory' and is shown in great detail in the movie. If you said what movie depicts my theory the best, I'd say this one does.

3. Patricia Cornwell.

- At 36, she was involved in a near fatal car accident when her life was spiralling out of control and it caused her to take stock and turn things around.

4. Barack Obama.

- At 24/36/48 involved in some form of health care issue, first at local, then state and finally federal level with the signing of Obamacare.

5. Mary Queen of Scots.

- At 24, she plotted to have her husband murdered and replaced with her lover, resulting in her losing her crown and becoming a prisoner for the rest of her life.

6. Charles Dickens.

- At 24, he hijacks a joint project with the famous illustrator, Robert Seymour, and produces his first breakthrough novel, *The Pickwick Papers*. He was accused by Seymour's widow of this leading to her husband's suicide.

7. Gail Sheehy.

- At 36, she writes her famous book *Passages*, by using the unpublished work of Roger Gould. Gould successfully sues her over this.

8. Erik Erikson.

- At 24, gets amazing transformation from failed artist turned art teacher, to meeting Anna and Sigmund Freud and learning psychoanalysis through being a patient.

- At 36, he began a study of adolescent Native Americans facing social change, which led to his term "Identity Crisis" (which is what he is most famous for).

- At 48, he published *Childhood and Society*, his first and most important book.

9. Muhammad Ali.

- At 36, he rebounds from a shock loss to the relatively unknown Leon Spinks by becoming the only heavyweight boxer to hold the title on three occasions. He also announces his retirement, i.e., he goes out on a high.

10. Nelson Mandela.

- At 36, he wins his reputation as a statesman, with the famous Freedom Address at the Kliptown conference.

- At 43, he decides to get involved in guerrilla activity by attacking some government buildings leading to his imprisonment.

Nearly every single "Significant Year" in his long life has been studied.

11. Prince William.

- At 24, he graduates as a military officer from Sandhurst.

- At 31, his seven-year career in the army ends and he struggles to find his new direction.

12. Humphrey Bogart.

- At 36, he has his breakthrough movie role in *The Petrified Forest*. His acting was called brilliant and compelling.

13. Charlie Chaplin.

- At 24, he begins his movie career after signing a contract with Keystone Studios.

- At 36, his movie *The Gold Rush*, became one the highest grossing films of the silent era and he says at the time, it is the film he wanted to be remembered by.

14. Spencer Tracy.

- At 36, he has his breakthrough movie *Fury*, and critics say his transformation is little short of miraculous.

15. Joe DiMaggio.

- At 36, injuries and poor form forced him into early retirement. Yet another case of the achievement material happening

- ...when he was 24, when he wins his reputation as 'The Yankee Clipper' (i.e., by Yankee Stadium announcer, Arch McDonald, comparing his big and high hitting to the new Pam Am airliner).

Just thought I'd throw that one in for good measure.

16. Marilyn Monroe.

- At 24, she was signed to a seven-year contract with 20th Century Fox, after successes with the films *All About Eve* and *The Asphalt Jungle*.

17. Amal Alamuddin.

- At 36, in addition to her wedding to George Clooney, she was appointed for five years to the UK International Law Panel and voted by Barbara Walters as 'Most Fascinating Person of the Year'.

18. George Clooney.

- At 36, he had a very poor reception for *Batman and Robin* and apologised for this years afterwards. He then had a major turnaround with *Out Of Sight* in the same year, declaring him to now be a star.

19. Jerry Seinfeld.

- At 36, *The Seinfeld Show* was properly launched and at 43, it ended.

20. Sir Tim Berners-Lee.

- At 36, he launched the world's first web page at CERN, which is what he was famous for and also suffered some initial negative press reports.

Another landmark example.

21. Charles Tiffany.

- At 36, he founded the Tiffany Jewelry company, after buying up all the diamonds he could in war-torn France and cornering the American market.

22. Arthur Wellesley.

- At 24, he began his military career after being rejected as a suitor because of his poor prospects.
- At 36, he leaves the military for a couple of years to commence a political career and also marries the same girl, who he had unsuccessfully proposed to at 24.

23. Brad Pitt.

- At 24, he had his first leading film role with *Dark Side of the Sun*.

- At 31, he had both critical and commercial success with *Seven*.

24. Angelina Jolie.

- At 36, she directs her first movie *In the Land of Blood and Honey*, which wins a Golden Globe and she receives honorary citizenship of Sarajevo.

- In addition, she is made a Special Envoy to the United Nations High Commission For Refugees.

25. John Cleese.

- At 24, gets discovered in America as a member of the *Cambridge Review*.

- At 36, *Fawlty Towers* is launched and becomes his biggest hit.

- At 48, *A Fish Called Wanda* is released and becomes a hit movie.

This is a perfect career sequence.

So here it is then, all laid out for you to recall and digest. Combined with the previous chapter, I have displayed for you the astounding correlations of major events with the "Significant Years" in so many, many lives. You have seen the 100% match of the major adult years (i.e., 24/36 and sometimes 48) with the randomly generated list of 25 recent celebrity deaths. You have seen the same result in even greater detail, with the objective list of 'The Ten Most Influential People of the Twentieth Century'. You have seen these high-profile cases backed up by a sample from the 40 daily obituary texts taken from newspapers, that appeared in Book One.

You have seen all the straightforward terminology used to describe facets of "Life Cycles Theory", which constitutes a brand new field of research. You have then seen a summary of the main purpose of this book, which is to display the truly intricate nature of the theory if you begin to combine individual lives, where there was some type of important relationship between them. Finally, you have seen all the ancillary supporting evidence that was included in the text, further displaying the universality of my evidence.

What I am about to conclude is just a logical extension of all the data presented. Yet it is a revolutionary statement, that has never been said before and challenges the very foundations of prevailing scientific and sceptical thinking. Are all these seemingly strange coincidences nothing more than a blip on the huge horizon of randomly distributed events...or is there a clearly demonstrated underlying simple structure to lives?

Is this, indeed, the first time anyone has shown that we are subject to a form of benign determinism, that lays out certain years as important turning points, based on a twelve-year symbolic cycle? While no-one can know the future, can we learn about what to expect in general terms based on a detailed life analysis? Can we also use this to assist our understanding of our key relationships, our life partners and best friends, our work colleagues, even our worst enemies?

I've intimated similar to this in Books One and Two, and now I want to take it one step further. This overwhelming evidence of "Life Cycles Theory" is suggestive of a second level of consciousness! Once again, it's not some out-there, unprovable concept. It's just being aware of the presence of the twelve-year cycle in your own life. It's not religious, or even occult, it's just common sense.

I call it "Superconsciousness" and I have written in detail about how it has impacted my life in Book Two. I use this disarmingly simple method of meditation on a weekly basis. No chants, no appeals to a conjectural higher power. Just a life review combined with integration of all past cycles. I am a constant guinea pig for this experiment and once again, I'm going to share it with you. Here's how it works.

As I am writing this I am currently less than one year away from my next "Significant Year", which will be a "Year of Broken Pathways". Readers of Book Two will know that I have researched and named this year, but I don't want to overburden you right now with yet more theory. Suffice it to say, I have a clear roadmap in my head, that some form of inexorable change is likely to occur soon and I even know what key period to expect it in.

I also do not know what this change will be. Given none of us like surprises, that may be both good or bad; I am a little apprehensive about it. To appreciate the process, all I have to do is look back at similar periods in my life in consecutive twelve-year periods and the answer seems crystal clear. At the exact same time in each twelve-year cycle, I also had no idea what was in store for me either.

I discover that the best way to describe my predicament is to say, "it's like a veil is drawn over the next period of time and it's not yet ready to be removed." I felt it strongly at my first adult age 19 "Year of Broken Pathways", when just before it, I had been enrolled in a science degree with the intention of doing a chemistry major, and though I had been a bit disenchanted, I was still studying for my half-yearly exams.

Then, to my surprise, I got turned around by a mixture of not being sure what I wanted and getting involved in a band and losing interest in formal study, but beginning to read about Freud and psychic research. It all emerged out the other side when I failed my annual exams and switched faculties to psychology.

The same process occurred at 31, when I became disenchanted with my job and appealed a promotion that I felt should have been mine. I have described this in earlier chapters. I came out the other side by doing a commercially-oriented graduate diploma and eventually becoming a management consultant.

It happened again, regular as clockwork, exactly twelve years later at almost the same time, when I learnt my parent company had been sold to a group of bankers, and I was once again disenchanted with this direction and it led me to buying out my partners and gaining total control of my destiny.

It happened the same way again twelve years later when I had downsized the company and was expecting a flow of work into the new year. Once again this did not occur and I closed the business, and at the same time realised I wanted to write about my theory, so first I should be doing a writing course.

Every time the subjective feelings were the same and the timing was the same. This will be the first time I approach the next such period with any understanding, however. What I am doing I refer to as "Living In Superconsciousness".

The further I look, in an analytic sense, the more I get the feeling that the real topic of the recurring symbolic twelve-year cycle is time itself. If "Living In Superconsciousness" is accessing the repetitive nature of events in our lives, then isn't this a totally new outlook on time?

Today we are flooded with exhortations to live in the present moment, to tune into a universal consciousness, and further than that the only thing that exists is the present. I am going to disagree with all of this. I am certainly not the first to maintain that the so-called present is just an illusion.

Marcelo Gleiser, the Appleton Professor of Natural Philosophy and Professor of Physics and Astronomy. who is also a recipient of the Presidential Faculty Fellows Award, summed up my argument better than I ever could,

> *"Take a look around. You may think that you are seeing all these objects at once, or 'now', even if they are at different distances from you. But you really aren't, as light bouncing from each one of them will take a different time to catch your eye. The brain integrates the different sources of visual information, and since the differences in arrival time are much smaller than what your eyes can discern and your brain process, you don't see a difference. The 'present' - the sum total of the sensorial input we say is happening 'now' - is nothing but a convincing illusion....*
>
> *'Now' is not only a cognitive illusion but also a mathematical trick, related to how we define space and time quantitatively. One way of seeing this is to recognize that the notion of 'present', as sandwiched between past and future, is simply a useful hoax. All that we have is the accumulated memory of the past — stored in biological or various recording devices — and the expectation of the future."*

I have used the term "Real Time" to suggest that living through the "Significant Years" with an understanding that they will be based on events in past cycles is a very special process. Indeed, in this book, I have suggested that living through periods of "Confluence" with an important relationship partner and knowing that you are doing it, will be called "Real Time Confluence". I use the phrase "Real Time", because it means anyone practicing it is integrating the past with the so-called present and the near future. They are integrating time itself.

As heretical as this sounds, I am being 19 and 31 and 43 and 55 all at once. It enables me to focus not on the present, but on the near future. This 'near future', however, is really just a symbolic replay of past cycles. Taken to its logical extreme, I am suggesting that time itself is cyclical and that the seemingly unstoppable flow of events we call 'the present' is just non-existent.

Of course, there is always more to tell, but I feel I've tested the absolute limits of most readers' desire for brand new revolutionary thinking. Keep in mind that everything is derived from and supported by my mass of biographical correlations. What you have seen is still only a fraction of what I could show you.

As a management consultant, I used to go by the maxim that you're only as good as your next piece of business, and for me now, this is my business. "Life Cycles Theory" is a living, breathing, brand new discipline and it supports not only the truth of the twelve-year cycle, but the concept called "Living In Superconsciousness" and the viewpoint that time itself is cyclical in a symbolic sense, just as our lives are cyclical in a symbolic sense.

I will return with my next book sooner rather than later, so until then, "may the cycles always bring you good fortune". Don't forget this book itself, just like all my books, is written in a cyclical and symbolic format, so just go back over them and even more will be revealed.

EPILOGUE

I've decided again to host a party for all my guests and announce just who gets the all-time "Confluent" couple award. This alone should bring out good numbers of attendees. In fact, I'm walking along the footpath just now, when I see a lovely picture of womanhood waving to me from the opposite side of the street. That flowing hair, those long legs and that shy, infectious smile could only belong to...someone I had written extensively about on Facebook and in my blogs, but who didn't make it into the book itself. Yes, it's Carly Simon, writer of that most intriguing song *You're So Vain*.

"Hey Neil, Neil. Can we have a word?"

"Of course, Carly. In fact, I was hoping that one day we would catch up."

"Yes, but you wrote all that stuff about me on Facebook and you never concluded it...and come to think of it, how come good old John Cleese gets a big section and I didn't get one? I mean, wasn't I interesting enough?"

"No, no. It's not that at all. No way was I going to leave you out, but you were such a strange case for "Confluence" that you didn't really fit the main section. Besides, what I wanted to say was, well, kinda personal. I think now's as good a time as any though. If you'd like me to, that is?"

"Oh yes, I want to find out how all this ends. Let's see, oh yes, you really did a good number on Willie Donaldson as the mystery man in *You're So Vain*. You know I wrote the book recently and said it was a combination of Warren and two more men."

"Look, I still don't buy Warren being the main act. Besides I've got you on the key evidence. *'Hat strategically dipped below one eye'*, like Willie was known for. *'When I was still quite naïve'*, like you were with Willie, rather than Warren and your breakdown afterwards...oh, and the kicker, *'some underworld spy or the wife of a close friend'*. Could only be, couldn't it?"

"Say, how'd you figure out all that? That I massaged the underworld spy thing for what I really wanted to say, which was underworld spiv."

"You said you did some massaging of the story and I'll bet that was to throw people off the scent, but I'm like Eliot Ness. Now what I really wanted to say was the reason I couldn't put you in the book; it was because of all the many, many lovers you've had, both famous and not-so-famous, you weren't "Confluent" with any of them, with one exception."

"No, can't be. How about James (Taylor), or Mick (Jagger), or Warren (Beatty), or Kris (Kristofferson), or Jeremy (Irons), or even Willie, or my current partner (Richard Koehler) for that matter?"

"Sorry, I've searched high and low. Boy, you've been a busy girl. The only case I could find was probably the least likely. You'll know when I tell you he's the subject of the song *Coming Around Again*."

"Oh, my other James (Jim Hart, her second husband for around 20 years). We were married quite a while and still are really good friends, but he was always gay and it took him some time to tell me."

"Yes, turns out he was born in 1950 and you two shared around eight months of "Partial Confluence". That explains the friendship angle of your relationship."

"Oh, so who am I "Confluent" with then, Neil? I mean I'm happy, I don't need anyone new in my life, but I'm just a little curious."

"The answer's in your birthday, Carly. You see it's also my birthday and I was born in 1950, as well as Jim. That would give us an amazing 100% "Partial Confluence". This, by itself, is no iron-clad guarantee that we would be friends, as we would have to form a reasonable bond. We have some common ground, I believe, with my music and psychology background. But alas, we're never likely to meet unless you're in Sydney and decide to have a swim at Bondi Beach. Let me know if you ever do."

"You're an interesting guy, that's for sure. So that's why you never put me in the main book. Ha! Say, can I come to this party you're throwing?"

"Of course, please join me and if you like rubbing shoulders with the famous then it should be a treat."

We enter the plush doors of an upmarket hotel ballroom to find this incredible array of suitably outfitted guests representing their various periods of history. There's so many, what with the recent celebrity deaths and famous couples. It's the couples we want to meet, but that's during the formal part when I properly introduce them.

Oh, and who should we meet first, but two impressively outfitted warriors from the days of Ancient Rome. None other than Scipio and Hannibal. I think they're discussing just who was the greatest-ever general.

"You know Hannibal, you managed to have the last word with me back in the court of Antiochus III, but now it's my turn to say that I always knew I had to be the greatest general after I beat you."

"Yes, but Alexander The Great never lost."

"Yes, but if he had faced me he would have almost certainly lost, because I know how to use an enemy's tactics against him like I did to you."

Oh, here comes Napoleon looking splendid in his full dress uniform.

"Gentlemen, gentlemen, I believe you are looking right now at the greatest general of all time. I conquered Europe in one day. No-one can match that."

Now the Duke of Wellington is drawn into the conversation.

"Yes, Napoleon, but if I conquered you, then I believe that title is mine."

Actually, this is only the beginning of this discussion I fear, so we'll leave them alone for a while. Oh, and who have we here, but Albert and Victoria in full ceremonial dress having a chat with William and Catherine.

"I believe we're both going to be finalists in this all-time "Confluent" couple award, isn't that right Albert, dearest?"

"Yes my love, but I fear this young couple of Royals may have some sort of edge, which I can't quite put my finger on. What does he mean when he says they're a poster couple?"

"Look, if you don't mind me saying so, your Royal Highnesses, but talking with you is really spooky, isn't it, darling?"

"Yes, William, I'm quite overwhelmed and just plain freaked out."

Why isn't that Humphrey Bogart and Lauren Bacall at the bar, with Spencer Tracy and Katharine Hepburn?

"Hey Neil. Come over here, buddy, and have a whisky, it'll get you relaxed before the speeches. Get him one, Sam, no make it a double."

"Um, couldn't I have a beer instead?"

"Nah, you've got to drink like a man. Say Spence and me think you're OK. Bit kinky round the edges, but you're basically on the money. I never knew that last bit about Kate. Man what a slap in the face."

"Guys I'd love to chat on, but I've got to meet some others as well, you understand."

I hear raised voices at this point and look over to see Liz Taylor, Richard Burton, Debbie Reynolds, and Zsa Zsa Gabor having a heated debate.

"Look, Debbie honey, you know I always felt guilty over stealing Eddie like that. I just had to leave you some jewellery in my will."

"You know you didn't have to Lizzie, darling."

"Ah forget about it, Lizzie. The moment I arrived on the set of Cleopatra, you knew you were a goner and Eddie was yesterday's man."

"Dahlinks, Dahlinks. You sink you inwented ze Hollyvood scandal. I had a much bigger scandal before you. I even had to be photographed viz a black eye to prove it."

"Who is this no talent rip-off of my scandal? Honey, do you remember they even called you the B-Side melodrama to me?"

"Vy of all ze nerve! Anyvay zere were two of you in love vis Richard only you fell out of love and he didn't."

"Ha. Nice one, Zsa Zsa. You've still got it."

I've got to move on, although part of me doesn't want to at the same time.

"Say, Carly, how are you enjoying it so far?"

"This is crazy cool! I know a whole bunch of A-listers, but this is another league. Let's meet some more."

Ah, here's an interesting person coming up to us. It's Carrie Fisher.

"Hi Carly, I believe we both made the same mistake of marrying a gay man. I mean, you were married a lot longer than me, when did you find out?"

"Oh yeah, well I found out early on he had this account with a gay club, but he apologised and I decided to believe him. Not the smartest move, I know."

"Sorry ladies, hate to break this up, but I've just seen a really interesting group that I've got to meet. It's Tom Cruise with Mimi Rogers, Nicole Kidman and Keith Urban, Katie Holmes and David Miscavige. Let's just say they're not having a barrel of laughs."

"Look here, Mimi, you started this whole unhappy saga when you introduced Tom to your father's corrupt version of our religion."

"Oh David come on, can't you see all the misery you've wrought with Tom's personal life. Am I right, Nicole? And how about you too, Katie?"

"Yes, when we made *Eyes Wide Shut,* it was a dreadful time in my life, but I'm so glad I came out the other end and met Keith. The lessons I learned then helped me understand Keith's own demons a little better."

"Now Mr. Killion, I've got to take you to task, sir. I'll have you know Tom's in a very good place now and your remarks are both unfair and unhelpful, and using a source such as Marty Rathbun, well let's just say he's been discredited. End of story."

"OK David, I hear your comment. If we just examine the biographical facts, you've got to admit a striking similarity between all three of Tom's marriage break-ups, whether or not Marty's public statements are accurate." At this point, Tom looks agitated.

"Guys, guys, guys. Hold on, this argument is beginning to sound like mission impossible to me. What's done is done. Let's leave it alone, OK?"

I beat a hasty retreat from that hornet's nest and try to gather my thoughts. Oh no, who should be coming my way but John Cleese flanked by all of his wives, past and present (with the exception of Alyce Eichelberger), as well as his mother.

"Ah Killion, I've cornered you at last. I took you to task on Facebook for writing a lot of drivel, but now I see you've pulled it all together. It's really rather good. Didn't think you'd hear me say that, did you?"

"Well no, John. Frankly, I'm shocked. I thought you'd think I was having a go at you, which I wasn't."

"I see you left some of the more embarrassing bits out, including my daughter. I've got to know though if 'poison' Alyce and I were the most "Confluent" then how come I've suffered so much grief?"

"Your problem with her, John, as I see it, was that you were too trusting. This one had an agenda and getting a big settlement was her main goal. The others were gracious. Anyway, unfortunately, there's no guarantees."

"You never did understand women, did you, my boy!"

"Look, mommy, I've had just about all I can take from you. Just, just go away will you."

With that, I think it's about time to get on with the main act, so I excuse myself and head backstage, where all the finalists are waiting. The band is warming up with *Unforgettable*, which sums up this night in a nutshell. I'm remembering the last time I did this and it didn't go as I had hoped. I'm a bit apprehensive all over again. I'm given my cue, it's too late now to back out.

"Well good evening ladies and gentlemen, to a night of awards devoted to couples. Yes, without each party's contribution to the whole, then things would not have turned out as they did. The brand new concept of "Confluence" was used to test so many famous couples, families, careers, and even worst enemies.

I've decided to announce the finalists for the category of best career-related "Confluence" first, and then best family-related "Confluence" and finally the big one, the best "Confluent" couple."

A voice from the audience is heard. It's William Shatner.

"Say Neil, how's about one for best friends, like Lenny and me?"

"Good point, William, but my problem was friendship ran across all the boundaries and is in the very definition of the concept itself. I didn't want to disappoint you two by having to include so many other cases in competition."

"Ah, OK I think. Anyway, you're a good schmoozer, Neil. I'll present that award myself."

Some laughter, but it's a pretty straight-faced audience.

"Alright, well let's get down to the finalists for the best career-related "Confluence". The first contestants just happen to be the world's best-known team, which are the astronauts for the 1969 Moon landing; Neil Armstrong, Buzz Aldrin, and Michael Collins."

There's a big round of applause for these guys.

"The second is Larry Page and Sergey Brin, the founders of Google, which a lot of you don't know, but everyone alive here tonight knows very well indeed. They wanted to store an immense amount of data and knowledge, and they've really delivered. Couldn't have done my research without them."

This also gets a fair round of applause.

"My last finalists are the legendary President Abraham Lincoln and his rival and good friend, General John J. Hardin. They seemed to intersect each other's lives at key points in their early careers."

Cheers from the crowd for the very tall Abe, which he acknowledged with an artistic wave of his hand.

"...and the winner is, Abraham Lincoln and John J. Hardin for the incredibly short time span of one month's "Confluence" to unearth the moment that changed both their lives." More cheers as they stepped forward and chants of "We want Abe. We want Abe." I duly hand him the microphone, which he declines with another cursory wave of his hand.

"Ah have no need for voice amplification, my boy." He stood erect with those famous hollow cheeks and coal black eyes. "Ah would just like to say, that ah'm truly honoured by this award, which is so deeply personal ta me. General Hardin was such a fine gentleman and adversary, that it troubled me greatly when he met an untimely death in battle, bein' so short a time after my first federal election victory, which put me on the national stage.

"I felt overwhelmed when ah met him tonight, and I wish everyone here would bury whatever hatchets they may have with others and just embrace. Goodnight and God Bless."

Wild cheering erupts. The hair on the back of my neck goes up. I regather my composure and proceed.

"Thank you, Mr. President, sir. Now to our next finalists, this time for the best "Confluence" in families award. The finalists are all most worthy of receiving this and I'll introduce them to you. Firstly, it's the Wright Brothers, who need no introduction as most everyone knows of them."

Loud cheering and chants of "Wilbur and Orville. Wilbur and Orville."

"Secondly, it's the equally famous Tiffany family of father, Charles and son, Louis. They became completely synonymous with their fields of diamonds and glassware, and are an outstanding example of mutual support."

More cheering, this time a couple of chants for "Charles and Louis."

"Finally, it's a family story of success, mixed in with fall-outs and crime, that finally ends in redemption and intersects with every shared "Year of Revolution". I give you 'Big Floyd' and 'Little Floyd' Mayweather."

There's some muted applause, but the Mayweathers are completely surprised.

"Say pop, what's going down right now?"

"Beats me, junior. Must say though, they look a bit outta shape to me. A quick million says none of 'em can go three rounds with you."

This time the laughter erupts and the chants begin, "Money Mayweather. Money Mayweather."

"I'm very pleased to announce that the winners in this category are the fabulous Tiffanys, Charles and Louis. They were the most "Confluent" and were born 36 years apart, and their whole careers and lives were intertwined, so that their successes were always shared."

On behalf of this duo, Charles comes forward to accept.

"Why Neil, this is quite an honour, in front of such a star-studded crowd. I, however, want to pay my respects to your own fabulous research, Neil, in that you managed to uncover the absolute pivotal moments in our combined lives.

"Yes, in war-torn Paris, in 1848, I put everything on the line to buy all the diamonds I could. From this singular moment in time came the company of today, which has shops in so many countries. Also with my son, Louis, you found the actual texts that proved your dates. Once again I am grateful. Thanks to everyone, this truly is the greatest gathering in history."

More cheers and a couple of chants for me. This is going way better than the first time. I feel really upbeat.

"Now for the big award of the night, the best "Confluent" couple award. With so many worthy couples, I've decided to double the number of finalists to six and I want to introduce them to you now.

"Firstly, we have Humphrey Bogart and Lauren Bacall, whose love story is legendary and the subject of song lyrics, and who are a wonderful example of "Confluence" in action."

There's a shout or two from around the bar and Bogart whispers to Lauren.

"Hey baby, this could be our night."

"Next we have our only living couple in Prince William and Catherine. They really began my whole line of research and are as well-suited as you could wish for."

Catherine grabs William's hand saying, "darling, this is making me feel really nervous."

"Couple number three needs no introduction, probably the best known Royal couple in British history, Queen Victoria and Prince Albert."

There's a ruffle of polite applause and Victoria acknowledges this with a restrained royal wave, while Albert nods.

"Next, we have a political couple with a tragic storyline because of an early death, that has been the subject of books, movies, and a musical. It's Juan and Eva Peron."

Quite a bit of loud applause and some shouts. They both wave enthusiastically to the audience without speaking.

"Following them, we have one of the twentieth century's best-known couples, President John F. Kennedy and Jackie. Their marriage was not exactly a bed of roses, but there's no denying their mutual support ran very deep."

A big round of applause and gasps of amazement to see them together.

"Finally, it's a couple not so well-known, but they displayed every aspect of "Confluence" in their improbable love story. It's the idol of the silent picture era, Charlie Chaplin, and his last wife, Oona O'Neill."

A small ruffle of applause and a bit of muted conversation.

"OK then. This is the moment you've been waiting for."

A small nudge from Bogie to Lauren, and a sly smile between Victoria and Albert.

"...and the overall winner is, Charlie Chaplin and Oona O'Neill."

A couple of audible gasps.

"Yes, not as famous as the others, but their rare 36-year age difference, combined with Chaplin's past exploits and the strength of the bonds of mutual support, combined with the instant attraction make them a truly standout couple."

At this, there is a very strange silent moment as Charlie adopts the famous walk of the tramp from his films and with Oona on his arm, accepts the award without a word being said.

Then the magical moment is broken with Queen Victoria turning to Albert and saying, "Come Albert, I think we've seen all of this charade that we're going to see. The nerve of our host granting the top place to a couple of unknown commoners is simply too much to bear." Albert nods in full agreement and they leave the stage.

Then a voice from the middle of the audience sings out. Why it's Brad Pitt, of all people.

"Hey Neil, I've got a question for you. Look, if you'd gotten us together last year, I guarantee Angelina and I would have been finalists and now look at us. It's all very well only being right after the facts, plus I'm not in a good place these days, so excuse me."

At this, both he and Angelina leave via separate doors, followed by George Clooney and Amal in a show of support.

Next, it's David Miscavige and Alyce Eichelberger, somewhat surprisingly leaving together and saying, "this whole thing is nothing but a rip-off." I suddenly get the same feelings of doom as I did last time. Time to make a statement.

"Well Brad's gone, but I would say to him and to all of you, I never pretended to be a mind reader. I don't know what'll happen next, any more than you do. That's why it's so much better to analyse a whole life than to see just part of the picture. Most importantly though, I hope you can see that "Life Cycles Theory" is not a belief system, it's the factual study of correlations, of important turning points in your life and a twelve-year cycle. It's certainly not a religion and though it's not quite a science like physics, it's a lot closer to it than anything else."

Then towards the back I see a familiar face jump to her feet. It's Joy Mangano.

"Neil, Neil. I just wanted to say, that whether you say it is belief or not, I believe you. What you described that can happen in your age 36 year is precisely what happened to me. Not just a year, a month or a day, but one single, mind-expanding moment changed my whole life forever. Not only that, but it's all on film in the movie of my life, Joy.

"Now you're right, I did massage some of the script, but not that bit. When my friend got on the phone after I'd blown my one big chance and asked me a sales question, well it was a miracle."

Now it's Patricia Cornwell who stands up.

"Yes, and the same for me too. When I lay dying in that car accident something fundamental happened to change my life on the spot."

Oh, now Emperor Napoleon stands up. I am almost overcome with joy.

"Yes, it's true, every last detail. When the sun broke through that heavy fog on our assault of the Pratzen Heights at Austerlitz, it was a miracle and they've written whole books about 'the sun of Austerlitz'."

I never thought he'd do this. Now it was Bogie from the stage.

"Yes buddy, when I read what you said about my breakthrough movie at the same time as Spence's and then how I met 'baby' (i,e., Lauren Bacall) in what you call a "Window of Opportunity", well I knew it was the real deal. Forget those walkers, it's their loss, I'm having a great time, so come on give us some music and keep the booze flowing. Let's hear it for Neil, everyone."

Cheers and applause all round. This time it really is different as people are less hesitant, plus there's so many of them, I can't count them all.

Well, it was a great after-party, but you know I can't give you all of the details. Suffice to say it did get pretty merry, if you know what I mean. At around 2.00 am, I excuse myself and leave by the back door. On the way out I bump into Francis Crick and James Watson.

"Great party, Neil. We were impressed by our own correlation and were disappointed not to be finalists. We were wondering, however, if it concerned you only having us celebrities to analyse? Plus were we like a big laboratory experiment to you, or did you genuinely like us?"

Good question, I mused to myself.

"Well, yes and no, is my equivocal answer. Once you've got a public profile, it's easy for a researcher to check a number of sources, to get as accurate and objective an account as possible. Plus I can sometimes get direct quotes, which are even better. But you're right, you are all part of a big laboratory experiment and though I am very grateful that most of you endorse what I do, I don't actually need your support.

"All lives matter to me, it's just so relatively hard for me to objectively study the lives of private citizens. You know, when a hotel bar manager said that at 36, she began her career by accident, when she was asked by a friend to pick up some glasses as a casual job, that was also very important to me.

"However, when a friend of mine couldn't see what I was on about when his own printed biographical summary said he commenced in business at 36, it also worried me. It wasn't the same business he was in now, but it was an important marker of change in his life. In any study I'd need to have access to some external material, rather than just rely on people's memory and personal interpretations.

"But to the last part of your last question, I must answer in the positive. I have absolutely loved getting to know the hidden corners of so many famous lives. I won't say I really liked you all, but I have so many stories that others have never heard of, not to mention your own, of course. Thanks for coming you two, I've got to leave now."

At that, I opened the heavy door and stepped outside on the pavement. I saw a lonely figure by a lamp post, and as I got closer I could see it belonged to the star of Book Two, Albert Einstein.

"Vell, vell, my boy, you are getting much closer to science than you sink. Not mere philosophy, not that zere's anything wrong with that, but ze accuracy of your "Year of Revolution" grows. Now I vant to know vat you sink about ze one mind-numbing moment, as you put it?"

"Well you know, Albert, there aren't many people I can talk to about that. Of course, I think it's so extraordinary as to be a field of study all on its own. I've even heard people speak anecdotally about a thought coming into their heads, that either defines their own future or the future of someone else who's 36. When the latter happens, I call them the "Agent of the Revolution". Plus, of course, if it is like a symbolic re-birth, then it could have some amazing implications."

"Yes, yes, my boy. I am pleased zat you seem to have advanced your theory since ve last spoke. Keep going, you're on ze right path."

"Thank you so much, Albert."

At this point, our conversation is interrupted by a limousine cruising by and stopping just in front of me. I excuse myself and open the front door. Then I suddenly notice who's driving. Why it's Gene Wilder complete with a chauffeur's cap.

"Wow, Gene. This is such a surprise. You're not the driver I was expecting."

"No, Neil. I'm sure I'm not. I just wanted to have a final word with you. You see I've been tuning into your "Superconsciousness" sessions and I know there's more that you haven't told us yet. Is that true?"

"Well yes, I guess it is, Gene. How'd you think to do that. You know, there was always such depth behind your sparkling blue eyes. I intuited that when I did your analysis."

"Yes, and you know what my guess is? My guess is that you haven't finished yet, but you can only tell us what it is you think we should know. When we're ready, there'll be more. Am I right?"

"Yes, Gene, you are. I haven't finished yet, that's for sure."

I settle back into the plush leather seat and feel a pleasant tiredness overtake me. I begin to close my eyes when all of a sudden, I am shaken awake by an insistent pair of hands and a playful laugh. It's Carly, who's been hiding in the back seat the whole time. She speaks to Gene.

"Hey driver, do you know the way to Bondi Beach?"

"Not really, Carly, but I think there's someone here who could help."